Twayne's English Authors Series

Sylvia E. Bowman, *Editor*

INDIANA UNIVERSITY

John Masefield

TEAS 209

John Masefield

JOHN MASEFIELD

By SANFORD STERNLICHT
State University of New York at Oswego

TWAYNE PUBLISHERS
A DIVISION OF G. K. HALL & CO., BOSTON

Library of Congress Cataloging in Publication Data

Sternlicht, Sanford V
  John Masefield.

  (Twayne's English authors series ; TEAS 209)
  Bibliography: p. 151 - 56.
  Includes index.
  1.   Masefield, John, 1878 - 1967—Criticism and interpretation.
PR6025.A77Z887   828'.9'1209   77-24770
ISBN 0-8057-6678-2

MANUFACTURED IN THE UNITED STATES OF AMERICA

71580

To Doe

It's not been done, the sea, not yet been done,
From the inside, by one who really knows;
I'd give up all if I could be the one. . . .

Dauber

Contents

About the Author

Sanford Sternlicht, professor and chairperson of the department of theatre at the State University of New York, College at Oswego, was formerly professor of English and Director of Graduate Studies in English at that institution.

A wide-range scholar-writer, Professor Sternlicht is the author of the following books: *Gull's Way* (poetry), 1961; *Love in Pompeii* (poetry), 1967; *The Black Devil of the Bayous* (history with E. M. Jameson), 1970; and *John Webster's Imagery and the Webster Canon* (literary criticism), 1972. His many articles on subjects from Shakespeare to Graham Greene have appeared in *Renaissance Papers, Papers on Language and Literature, Minnesota Review, Harvard Magazine, Florida Review, College English, Ball State Forum, Midwest Quarterly, The Calcutta Review, Studies in Humanities, Writers Digest,* etc. His poetry has appeared in over three hundred publications throughout the world including the *New York Times,* the *New York Herald Tribune, Christian Science Monitor, Saturday Evening Post, Canadian Forum, Dalhousie Review,* and *Poetry Review* (London).

Preface

More than almost any other writer, John Masefield outlived his contemporary critical reputation. He was a Georgian relic in the Nuclear Age. As a result of his adhering to traditional forms, he lost the attention of critics to more iconoclastic writers and as the reading public turned to more exciting novels, Masefield became one of the most underrated of major twentieth-century writers. Nevertheless, certain of his early sea poems have become part of the permanent anthology of read, loved, and prized English poetry. Unfortunately, his best work, the long narrative poems of the 1911 - 1921 period, is out of fashion. This book, written in the hope of reviving general reader and critical interest in a fine, enjoyable poet, is the first in-depth study of Masefield's entire canon that has as yet been undertaken after his death. An understanding and evaluation of the totality of Masefield's accomplishment is long overdue, for as a literary artist he wrote not only lyric poetry and narrative verse but he prolifically produced novels, plays, stories, histories, books of literary criticism, essays, reviews, biographies, autobiographies, addresses, prefaces and postscripts.

The first chapter of this book has proved to be particularly difficult because no biographies of John Masefield exist. He did not desire one to be written while he was alive nor did he wish for someone to write his life after his death. Despite his copious autobiographical writings, he seems to have obfuscated the facts of his youth. For Masefield, the artist's life was unimportant; only his work mattered. Thus the first chapter of this book required much investigation, sorting, and integration. It now stands as the longest, most comprehensive, most accurate biography of John Masefield in print.

Chapter 2 treats the sea poet of the famous lyrics, "Sea-Fever" and "Cargoes." Chapter 3, perhaps the most important chapter in this book, is concerned with Masefield's ultimate artistic contribution: his long narrative poems from *The Everlasting Mercy* through *King Cole* with particular emphasis on the first-mentioned work and on *Dauber* and *Reynard the Fox*. Chapter 4 deals with the remainder of Masefield's poetry and in particular with the fine poems "August 1914" and "The Wanderer." The fifth chapter evaluates Masefield as a dramatist. In the period of his friendship with John Millington Synge, he took his playwrighting most seriously; and his *Tragedy of Nan*, produced by Harley Granville-Barker, was a critical success. Eventually Masefield realized that his talent was not theatrical although his long verse narratives, like Robert Browning's, are quite dramatic. Finally, and without bitterness, Masefield withdrew from the theater and limited himself to experimental closet drama.

In the sixth chapter Masefield's novels, which range from the banal to the excellent, are evaluated; for his novels replaced his long narrative poems as the medium of his story telling. Chapter 7 deals with Masefield's non-fiction, especially with his magnificent epic history, *Gallipoli*. Lastly, Chapter 8 evaluates Masefield's literary career as England's most popular Poet Laureate.

I am particularly indebted to two writers who have written about John Masefield with sensitivity and justifiable admiration: Muriel Spark, whose *John Masefield* was published in 1953, and the poet's most dedicated and persistent American admirer, Fraser Bragg Drew. Despite an almost complete critical disinterest in Masefield's writing, much of his work has remained in print: the sea poems, the children's books, the early essays, the naval histories, and one or two of the sea novels. Hopefully, my study of Masefield will not only send readers eager for a fresh experience of the literature of the first half of this century to Masefield, but will also provide background for understanding and appreciation to those who somehow have come across a pleasing novel or a moving poem by Masefield and who wish to know more about the work of an old sailor who wrote so well and so passionately about the sea.

SANFORD STERNLICHT

State University of New York
at Oswego

Acknowledgment

Permission kindly has been granted by The Macmillan Company to quote from the works of John Masefield.

Chronology

1878   John Edward Masefield born June 1, at Ledbury, Herefordshire; son of George Edward and Carolyn Parker Masefield.

1880   Solicitor father and mother die.

1888   Reared by aunt and uncle.

1889 -   Sent to King's School, Warwick. Unhappy, runs away,
1891   found and returned.

1891   September 23, sent to merchant service training ship H.M.S. *Conway*, moored in the Mersey, Liverpool.

1894   Apprentice on windjammer sailing around Cape Horn to Chile.

1895   April, Sixth Officer of White Star Line's *Adriatic*. Left ship in New York.

1895 -   Rode the rails hobo class to California and back. Tended bar.

1897   in Luke O'Connor's Columbian Hotel saloon in Greenwich Village, then moved to Yonkers to work in carpet factory.

1897   July, returned to England.

1900   November 5, met and befriended by William Butler Yeats.

1902   *Salt Water Ballads* (poetry).

1903   January, met John Millington Synge at Bloomsbury apartment of William Butler Yeats.

1903   Married Constance de la Cherois-Crommelin of Ireland. *Ballads*.

1904   Six months on the *Manchester Guardian*.

1905   *A Mainsail Haul* (prose stories and sketches). Daughter Judith born.

1907   *A Tarpaulin Muster* (prose stories and sketches).

1908   *Captain Margaret* (novel).

1909   *The Tragedy of Nan and Other Plays*.

1910   *The Tragedy of Pompey the Great* (play). *Ballads and Poems*. Son Lewis born.

1911   *The Everlasting Mercy*. (narrative poem). *Shakespeare* (criticism).

1912   *The Widow in the Bye Street* (narrative poem).

1913   *Dauber* (narrative poem). *The Daffodil Fields* (narrative poem).

1914   *Philip the King* (play).

1915   *The Faithful* (play). August, commanded evacuation boat for wounded at the Dardanelles under British Red Cross. Ill with fever.

1916   January, began lecture tour of United States for British war effort. March, returned to England to write *Gallipoli* (history), *The Old Front Line* (history), *Good Friday* (play), *Sonnets and Poems.*

1917   With British Red Cross in France. *Lollingdon Downs* (poetry).

1918   January, second tour of United States. Doctor of Letters, Yale University; Doctor of Laws, Harvard University.

1919   *The Battle of the Somme* (history). *Reynard the Fox* (narrative poem).

1920   *Right Royal* (narrative poem). *Enslaved* (narrative poem).

1921   *King Cole* (narrative poem).

1922   Doctor of Letters, Oxford University; Doctor of Laws, University of Aberdeen.

1923   *A King's Daughter* (play). Doctor of Letters, Manchester University. Romanes Lecture at Oxford.

1924   *Sard Harker* (novel).

1925   *William Shakespeare* (criticism).

1926   *ODTAA* (novel).

1927   *Tristan and Isolt* (play).

1929   *The Hawbucks* (novel).

1930   Appointed Poet Laureate by King George V. *The Wanderer of Liverpool* (poetry and prose). Doctor of Letters, Liverpool; Doctor of Laws, St. Andrews. Freedom of Hereford.

1931   *Chaucer* (criticism).

1933   *The Bird of Dawning* (novel).

1934   *The Taking of the Gry* (novel).

1935   Order of Merit. *Victorious Troy: or The Hurrying Angel* (novel).

1936   *Eggs and Baker* (novel).

1938   *Dead Ned* (novel).

1939   *Live and Kicking Ned* (novel).

1940   *Some Memories of W. B. Yeats* (poetry and prose).

1941   *In the Mill* (autobiography). *The Nine Days Wonder* (history).

1942	Lewis Masefield killed in action.
1943	*Wonderings. Between One and Six Years* (autobiographical poetry).
1944	*New Chum* (autobiography).
1949	*On the Hill* (poetry).
1952	*So Long to Learn* (autobiography).
1960	February 18, Constance Masefield died.
1961	*The Bluebells and other Verse.*
1965	*Old Raiger* (poetry).
1966	*In Glad Thanksgiving* (poetry). *Grace Before Ploughing* (autobiography).
1967	May 12, John Masefield died in his home: Burcote Brook, Abingdon, Berkshire.
1967	June 20, ashes of John Masefield interred in the Poets' Corner, Westminster Abbey.

CHAPTER 1

The Wanderer

JOHN Masefield, a country child who went to sea, came ashore again in a few years; but he never lost his love for deep water, for the hard challenging life of the sailor, and for the beauty of a ship with wings of canvas that sailed to the horizon like a great white bird. Most important for his creative imagination, he never lost a childlike sense of wonder at the unfolding adventures and possibilities of life. This *joie de vivre* helped make him one of the most popular and "most loveable of English writers."[1]

Despite the fact that Masefield wrote three autobiographical books, *In the Mill* (1941), *New Chum* (1944), and *So Long to Learn* (1952), as well as two long autobiographical poems, *Biography* (1912) and *Wonderings* (1943), the events of his early life and of his private life remain, as he wished, obscure. His autobiographical writings are for the most part creative histories of the development of his poetic imagination and not chronicles of his life. Although Masefield has written more words about himself than any other twentieth-century English author, we know less about his life, especially the first thirty years, than we do about any other major literary figure of the period.

In *Biography,* Masefield scores the listing of dates and events in the life of a writer: "When I am buried, all my thoughts and acts / will be reduced to lists of dates and facts. . . ." Rather, he wished to have his future biographer know that

> By many waters and on many ways
> I have known golden instants and bright days;
>
> . . . .
>
> The dawn when, with a brace-block's creaking cry,
> Out of the mist a little barque slipped by,

and that he had also been given "The gift of country life, near hills and woods / Where happy waters sing in solitudes." In other words, Masefield tells us in *Biography* that the important events in his life are not those listed in *Who's Who* or in *Contemporary Authors;* they are the times he saw lovely and graceful ships, like the *Wanderer,* returning to Liverpool; enjoyed the inspiring conversations and moments of deepest communication with friends like William Butler Yeats and John Millington Synge; and experienced the sacred minutes when the courage or sacrifice of men at sea or at war was revealed like an epiphany to a poetic understanding. Undated but happy moments, these are "The days that make us happy make us wise." As for the rest,

> Print not my life or letters; put them by:
> When I am dead let memory of me die.
> Blessed be those who in their mercy heed
> This heartfelt prayer of mine to Adam's seed;
> Blessed be they, but may a curse pursue
> All who reject this living prayer, and do.
>
> ("Sweet Friends.")

Nonetheless, Masefield's anniversaries, milestones, and honors need recording if only to serve as the skeleton to the fully formed flesh of understanding; for John Masefield—neither a Bohemian exile nor a recluse—was an artist who helped shape and was shaped by his time.

I *Childhood and Apprenticeship*

John Edward Masefield was born in Ledbury, Herefordshire, on June 1, 1878. Masefield himself was not quite sure, however, of the exact place or date; but he was satisfied to speak of "in or near" and "on, or nearly on" when he wrote *So Long to Learn*.[2] Ledbury town records indicate, however, that he was born there on the above date in a house known as "The Knapp."[3] His parents were solicitor George Edward and Carolyn Louisa Parker Masefield. The poet's mother died on January 20, 1885, and his father died shortly afterward. Masefield was taken to The Priory, Ledbury, formerly his grandfather's house which had become the home of an aunt and uncle; and he resided there until 1888 when he was sent to King's School, Warwick.

In Masefield's biographical works, he chose not to speak of his parents or of their early death during his childhood. He preferred to write about his first mental and sensual impressions: "All of my earliest memories are of intense delights. Some of these were of the country: many were of the waters; many others are of birds and flowers, of strange things seen and romantic impressions given, of customs and ways about to pass from use."[4] Thus Masefield indicates that, from the beginning of his conscious existence, he was intensely interested in water, in country life, and in the passing of crafts and customs. To these he apprenticed his life through work, craft, and art and by means of thought, sentiment, and nostalgia.

In *Wonderings*, Masefield recollected his first six years of life in verse that was much like William Wordsworth's *The Prelude* in its intent if not in its meter. His Ledbury was "a little town of ancient grace,"[5] and the poet recalled

> Two fields to the canal, and then
> A farm, a mill, and fields agen,
> A wood, with yew trees almost black;
> A bridge with railways on its back;
> A line of poplar-trees, a white
> Steep, hilly roadway just in sight;
> A hill, of which the stories told
> That it had moved in days of old,
> Glid for two days, church, manor, village,
> Pump, barton, tavern, crop, and tillage.[6]

When Masefield was seventy-two years old, the city of Hereford, which was some dozen miles from his native Ledbury, granted him "The Freedom of the City." In accepting the honor, Masefield said, "I am linked to this Country by subtle ties, deeper than I can explain: they are ties of beauty."[7] He never could forget the bountiful and beautiful agricultural land of his childhood: "I was born in this County. . . . I passed my childhood looking out on these red ploughlands and woodland and pasture and lovely brooks, knowing that Paradise is just behind them. I have passed long years thinking on them, hoping that by the miracle of poetry the thought of them would get me into Paradise, so that I might tell the people of Paradise, in the words learned there, and that people would then know and be happy."[8]

Masefield's early experience with literature came with the stories told or read to him by his nurse. The fare was what would be expected in a middle-class Victorian home; even *Dick Whittington and His Cat* was introduced.[9] Tennyson's *The Dying Swan* was one of the boy's earliest delights; and, having been taught to read before his sixth birthday, he read and committed to memory copious amounts of Longfellow, especially *Hiawatha* and *Evangeline.*[10] Since Masefield's most significant contribution as a literary artist would be as a superb storyteller and since he would be "the last major narrative poet using English,"[11] the importance of his early exposure to and delight in the narrative poetry of the nineteenth century cannot be overestimated.

Near his second home, The Priory, was the churchyard and church of Ledbury with its Gothic bell tower which the young boy climbed as he later did tall masts. In the tower he hid and read books from his grandfather's library or climbed onto the roof and gazed upward at the spire to the golden weathercock. Although Ledbury Church was immortalized in *The Everlasting Mercy* (1911), the bells of this church were one of the young Masefield's chief delights; indeed, he willingly suffered the torment of interminable Victorian Sunday sermons because of the ecstatic sound of the bells. In 1951, Masefield published an essay titled *The Ledbury Scene As I Have Used It In My Verse* in a limited, signed edition; and the proceeds were used to repair the bell tower and to restore the bells. The essay reveals the importance of Herefordshire, Ledbury, and Ledbury Church to his creative art; they gave him "the three good things of life, 'good air, good water, and good bells.' "[12]

Despite subsequent adventures and experiments in the realms of vegetarianism, theosophy, and agnosticism, it can safely be said that Masefield never really strayed very far from his church; it was always with him whether he realized it or not. And, as to his home town, Ledbury is to be found in *The Everlasting Mercy*, in *The Widow in the Bye Street* (1912), in *The Daffodil Fields* (1913), in *Reynard the Fox* (1919), and in other poems; and the English countryside settings abound in his poems, novels, and plays.

Masefield's deep interest in fox-hunting, which ultimately came to fruition in *Reynard the Fox* and in the "country novels" such as *The Hawbucks*, also stemmed from his Ledbury childhood:

My own interest in fox-hunting began at a very early age. I was born in a good hunting country, partly woodland, partly pasture. My home, during my first seven years, was within half a mile of the Kennels. I saw hounds on most days of my life. Hounds and hunting filled my imagination. I saw many meets, each as romantic as a circus. The huntsman and whipper-in seemed, then, to be the greatest men in the world, and those mild slaves, the hounds, the loveliest animals.[13]

When the time arrived for an education that was more formal than his aunt's tutelage, young John was sent to the King's School, Warwick; but the sensitive, introspective orphan was so thoroughly miserable in the atmosphere of the boarding school that he ran away, had to be found, and was then returned. After his aunt and uncle despaired of additional formal education for their difficult young ward, they decided that a seaman's life as a merchant marine officer might be the answer to John's and their problem. Anyway, this life would remove him from underfoot and introduce him to the floating merchant-marine schools that were run by the government to provide the apprentice officers that were greatly needed on British ships. On the holystoned white decks of one of these, the H.M.S. *Conway*, an ex-ship-of-the-line that was moored in the Mersey off Liverpool, John Masefield met the sea and its ways for the first time in September, 1891. At the age of thirteen he was not only removed from the pleasant, middle-class country life to which he had been born, but also from the leisurely Classical education to which he had been exposed. He was suddenly thrust below decks in a damp, dark, ancient man-of-war that was packed with hundreds of hustling boys and men who spoke almost a different language—the language of seamen—and who were engaged in learning a difficult, tasking, practical craft.

Masefield grew to love the sea, the *Conway*, and the sailors' ways. In 1933, he wrote *The Conway*, a history of the Mersey training ships, all ex-warships, which sequentially bore the name Conway. And in 1944 Masefield published *New Chum*, a delightful and moving account of his first term aboard H.M.S. *Conway* from September through December, 1891. The fledgling apprentice seamen were all called "new chums" and Masefield took great joy in the newfound camaraderie of ship's boys. During this school term, the thirteen-year-old lad learned the pleasure one could give one's fellows by skillfully telling stories, and he returned stories for the friendship of a senior lad whom he hero-worshipped. Masefield recalled the senior's "name" as "H. B":

He waggled a brief message, then straightened his bedding, and turned in. "Now, then chum," he said, "do you know any ghost yarns?"
As it happened, I knew many of different kinds, possibly some hundreds, with which I had scared my childhood whenever I had had the chance. I said that I knew some. "Right, then," he said. "Heave round and tell me some." He settled his pillow on the edge of his hammock, and turned towards me. With some care, lest I should fall on deck, I turned towards him and began my ghost yarn.[14]

Masefield's first experience as a storyteller came therefore, in service to his fellow students. When H. B.'s orders arrived, Masefield was broken hearted because he was losing his first true friend: "The news laid me low. H. B. would be gone on the morrow. . . . I had been a grubby little new chum, yet he had let me spin him ghost yarns. . . . He had been kind and wise and friendly; and now he was going, and tomorrow night he would not sling next me, and ask for a really good ghost."[15]

The young storyteller wanted to tell his hero one last story, a tale he considered to be the finest in his repertoire: "I made ready the best ghost stories still in my collection, in case he might like them. He came down to his hammock very late; almost everybody was asleep. He was sad as he undressed. 'It's sad. saying all these good-byes,' he said. I knew only too well how sad. I asked if he would like a yarn. He said: 'No, thanks very much; it's very late, now. We should wake the sleepers, and that's what sailors must not do. Good night.' "[16] Although Masefield's finest ghost story was untold, he spent the rest of his life telling stories to his missing friend whom he never saw again, although he later tried to locate "H.B." and follow his career. The orphan's loss of his substitute father-brother was so terrible that almost fifty-five years later Masefield wrote that "Nothing in my boyhood hurt me so cruelly as the loss of H.B."[17] Although "H.B." disappeared, possibly lost at sea like so many of Masefield's early companions, he lived throughout Masefield's life as a shadowy viewer and critic of the poet's work. "I do not know what became of him; but I have thought of him every day for more than half a century."[18]

During his first term at the Merchant-marine school, Masefield saw the clipper ship *Wanderer*, a beautiful but ill-fated vessel. Later, he described this ship in the poems *Ships* and *Biography*, and in 1930 he wrote her history in prose in *The Wanderer of Liverpool*. The ship "remained a symbol to the poet of grace and power and nobility of effort in spite of failure."[19] Masefield thought its name seemed to fit him as well as the sailing vessel; he would be a wanderer not only around the world in his youth but also through the world of poetry: "I liked the name, the *Wanderer*. It struck into my mind as a name of beauty, as a sort of seagull of grace there. The *Wanderer* . . . the more I thought of the name, the more wonderful it seemed. It suggested skies of desolation, with a planet; seas of loneliness, with that ship in sail."[20]

The *Wanderer* left that autumn on a disastrous voyage. She met a vicious storm, was badly mauled, and had to limp home, and became a symbol of wounded but proud beauty. Young Masefield, who was on deck in the *Conway* when a great cry arose in the harbor, "The *Wanderer!* The Wanderer!," was breathless at the sight:

The *Wanderer* came out of the greyness into sunlight as a thing of such beauty as the world can seldom show. She was in the act of preparing to dock with tugs, sidling, so that I saw her slowly come forward and turn away. She had been lopped at all her cross-trees, and the wreck of her upper spars was lashed in her lower rigging. As she turned, her tattered sails (nearly all were tattered) suddenly shone all over her; her beautiful sheer, with its painted ports, shone. I had seen nothing like her in all my life, and knew, then, that something had happened in a world not quite ours.[21]

All through his creative life Masefield particularly admired beauty in defeat and those human beings who, like King Lear, achieved a special state of grace through courage, endurance, and perseverance despite the decisions of an ill-disposing fate. Such people included the men and women of Troy; King Arthur and his knights; Tristam; the young heroes of *Sard Harker* (1924), *ODTAA* (1926), and *The Bird of Dawning* (1933); and the contemporary English heroes of *Gallipoli* (1916) and *The Nine Days Wonder* (1941). As Muriel Spark has stated, "It will be observed, time and again in the poet's writings, how invariably he finds an exalted beauty in the symbol of great, though defeated, endeavor."[22]

Masefield obtained his first copy of Robert Louis Stevenson's *Treasure Island* on the *Conway* and was soon enraptured by the possibility that such South Sea adventures might overtake him. Alas, he could not then realize that the day of the clipper ship was nearly over, that he and his young fellows were being trained in the techniques of mid-nineteenth-century sailing, and that the twentieth century was to be the age of the "Dirty British coaster with a salt-caked smoke stack. . . ." Masefield's overriding nostalgia that appears in so much of his work stems not only from his earliest exposure to the old country life in Ledbury but also from his archaic training for service in wind-driven, square-rigged vessels.

His second term on the *Conway* found Masefield under the tutelage of the old master seaman Wallace Blair, who taught knots and splices to the apprentices and who also tended the many ship's oil lamps below decks.[23] Blair, who had spent thirty years at sea in famous vessels, was also a master "yarn spinner of the old dog-watch kind."[24] Because of Blair's stories about the adventures and the tragedies of clipper ships, young Masefield felt "that in a ship the spinning of yarns was almost a part of the craft."[25] Blair's legends of daring and defeat became a part of Masefield's sea tales that appeared not only in the early collections of his prose—*A Mainsail Haul* (1905), which he dedicated to Blair's memory, and *A Tarpaulin Muster* (1907)—but also in his novels and in his long narrative poem, *Dauber* (1913). And, like Dauber, young Masefield on the *Conway* was trying unsuccessfully to draw and to paint nautical scenes.[26] Unknowingly, Masefield was being apprenticed to his chosen profession, storytelling, as well as to the craft of seamanship. He needed, however, the practical experience of voyages and of work on the ocean, for not men but "The sea creates stories."[27]

Already, even before his first assignment at sea, the young apprentice conceived the idea of becoming a professional writer; and this intention conflicted with his equally strong desire to follow the sea as a career:

I had hoped to be a writer, that is, if you can call wild dreams of some day being able to write, a hope. Unformed dreams of the sort had sometimes been in me, had been perceived in me, and had been mocked, with energy and with system: "What? You a writer? How can you be a writer? Only clever people are writers: and terrible lives they lead, both in this world and the next."

Well, if I could not be a writer (and the door to that garden seemed final-ly slammed) could I be a teller of stories? Here was Wally, a born story-teller, delighting all hearers with his stories. Why should not I be content to be such another, a yarn spinner, a solace in the second dog-watch? I asked myself this, having no other to ask, and the answer came flooding back, that to be a story-teller was only a part of my want. I had hoped to know a great many books, to know a great deal of knowledge, and to tell all sorts of stories in all sorts of ways.[28]

After Masefield had completed his second year on the *Conway*, he was shipped out as an apprentice aboard a windjammer bound round Cape Horn for Chilé: but along the way he had shore leave in 1894 in the Argentine. January, 1895, found Masefield Sixth Of-ficer of the White Star Line's *Adriatic;* and, when the ship reached New York, Masefield fell in love with that city. It was for him then and all his life "a gladness, that romantic, beautiful, exciting city, the Queen of all romantic cities, with such sparkle in her air and in her people."[29] On April 9, 1895, he decided to leave his ship with five dollars and his sea-chest and remain in New York; for, significantly, he "found that the faculty of mental story telling had returned. . . ."[30]

When the seventeen-year-old seaman entered Mr. Pratt's bookstore on Sixth Avenue near Greenwich Avenue, he bought his first volume of Sir Thomas Malory's *Morte d'Arthur;* with this he began his career of serious reading as well as his devotion to pre-Renaissance English literature. He obtained a job as a combination porter, bar boy, and jack-of-all-trades in Luke O'Connor's Columbian Hotel saloon on Greenwich Avenue and Christopher Street. He worked sixteen hours a day for ten dollars a month. At 2 or 2:30 A.M. his work done, Masefield would take a glass of whiskey to his garret above the saloon and read Malory until his eyes shut with exhaustion.

Four months later, an acquaintance of his obtained a better job for Masefield with a starting wage of $1.05 a day[31] in a carpet factory, the Moquette Mill on the Saw Mill River Road in Yonkers. And so on a September morning the ex-seaman took the "El" to 155th Street and the New York Central train to Yonkers, some twenty minutes away. Masefield rather enjoyed working in the factory doing a variety of production-line chores. For a while, he considered remaining in Yonkers and making a career of a factory job—easy work compared to standing watch around the clock on a bucking windjammer. When his salary was increased to $8.50 a week, the teen-ager felt so prosperous that, after he had discovered a bookstore with a most sympathetic thirty-year-old owner, William Palmer East, Masefield habitually purchased a book each Friday evening and read it over the weekend. Among the first purchases was a seventy-five-cent copy of Chaucer; and that evening, as he recalled "I stretched myself on my bed, and began to read *The Parliament of Fowls;* and with the first lines entered into a world of poetry until then unknown to me."[32] As a result, Masefield's study of poetry deepened; and Chaucer, John Milton, Percy Bysshe Shelley, and John Keats became his mentors. Shelley converted the impressionable youth to vegetarianism; he thought the practice brought him a clearness of mind that he had never previously experienced.[33] Unfortunately, Masefield overdid vegetarianism by abjuring milk; and, weak from lack of protein, he finally gave up the regimen.

Most important of all, Masefield began to write verse, and in this respect he was encouraged by East. After two years in Yonkers, the youth reluctantly decided to relinquish his secure factory job and return to England. At first, he had flirted with the idea of studying to become a physician; but his early attempts at poetry convinced him that "my law was to follow poetry, even if I died of it."[34] He always longed for the sea and missed the orderly life of the seafarer, as well as the daily opportunity to commune with nature; but he knew that he had to surrender everything for a new apprenticeship to the craft of writing. Leaving almost everything behind him, Masefield returned to New York City; some *Conway* chums arranged his passage home; his American Idyll ended on July 4, 1897; but his love for this country remained constant all his life.

II   *The Writer Emerges*

Masefield, who had grown homesick for England, wanted to be in his native land when Queen Victoria celebrated her Diamond Jubilee. Englishmen from all over the world were returning as if they somehow sensed that their nation had reached its high-water mark in history and that the tide was about to turn. It was still Victorian England, and the novels of Charles Dickens and the new works by Robert Louis Stevenson held sway. Dante Gabriel Rossetti and his fellow Pre-Raphaelite, William Morris, represented the current popular voices in English poetry. Was there any room for a poet with a relatively sparse and somewhat self-provided education? Would there be an audience for a poet who still spoke and loved the difficult, pragmatic, technical, ancient, and rough language of the sea? These were the questions in the young sailor's mind as he made his way to London to find lodgings and friendship in Bloomsbury. Searching for literary and artistic friends, but shy and defensive about his country and nautical dialect, he was described as "a quiet youth with eyes that seemed surprised at the sight of the world, and hair that stood up behind like a cockatoo's feather."[35] His air was serious and nautical and romantic; his voice was deep and solemn; his look of surprise never left him and almost every writer who met Masefield commented about it.

Seventeen years old, Masefield was too ill and too poor for school, so that all he could do was to read and to haunt the reading room of the British Museum. Fortunately, country byways were not so far from London as they are now, for the youth was able to wander from the city from time to time for fresh air and to draw much needed spiritual nourishment from a life simpler than city commerce: "I soon found I could walk right out of London on the north and west. This was a great joy to me; it made London seem much less like a prison."[36] Although Rossetti, Algernon Swinburne, and Morris continued to hold Masefield's attention, he began the study of Matthew Arnold and of Elizabethan dramatists. After reading their plays and after imagining the effects of their most striking scenes, he began to consider writing drama as well as poetry.

Masefield's first years in London were so difficult as a struggling writer that he never wished to discuss them; they were, he wrote in *Biography*, "Years blank with hardship." Speaking of future biographers, he said: "So, if the penman sums my London days/ Let him but say that there were holy ways,/ Dull Bloomsbury streets of dull brick mansions old. . . ." Bloomsbury provided his "college," and his enjoyment of intellectual companionship eased the pain of poverty.

In the fall of 1899, Masefield read a short piece of prose that may have been the single most important reading of his life. When the London *Daily Chronicle* published a review of William Butler Yeats' *Poems*, Masefield, who then knew very little about the thirty-four-year-old Irishman, thought that the review "was the work of a rare and generous understanding. . . ."[37] As a result of the review, he purchased the book, read Yeats' poetry and became his life-long disciple.[38] After reading everything by Yeats that he could find, Masefield was surprised that the poet's early Celtic narratives which had been written when he was still in his teens could havesuch force, such grace, and such an exquisite and matchless style. Only twenty-one himself, Masefield began to write poems and stories based primarily on his own experiences while at sea; he did so with as much measured artistry and inventiveness in the Yeatsian fashion as he could evoke; and the magazines began to accept his work.

On November 5, 1900, Masefield met and was befriended by Yeats who was then living and holding court in Bloomsbury.[39] Members of the court included Lady Gregory, A.E. (George Russell), Lionel Johnson, and, most important of all for Masefield, John Millington Synge. Yeats' lodging became Masefield's shrine: "Perhaps no-one of us within the room / But felt that any beauty might begin / At any moment there. . . ."[40] The room, located at

18 Woburn Buildings, Bloomsbury, was on the second floor above a noisy slum; but Masefield speaks in *Biography* of the remembered room as a place "Where there was wine and fire and talk with some / Under strange pictures of the wakened soul. . . ."

As years passed, Yeats' poetry became more symbolic, more profound, more experimental, more universal; but Masefield, especially after the Laureateship, seldom strayed from Edwardian forms, from very English subjects, and from somewhat more superficial themes. However, Masefield continued to write about the older poet with the greatest of admiration, respect, gratitude, and affection; for, despite the many hardships of Masefield's early life, he never developed a fierce sense of competition as a writer, a vituperativeness toward those who did not share his artistic ideas, nor a psychological need to found a school of poetry or to establish an Utopia. Somehow this gentle poet, despite the rough language of his narratives, remained truer to his deeply felt Christian values and to his love of mankind than most of his contemporaries who came to art from affluence.

Another writer very important to Masefield, John Millington Synge, he met at one of Yeats' Monday night soirées in January, 1903. Masefield admired the Irish playwright's gustiness, his vivaciousness, and his deep commitment to life. The two men remained friends until Synge's death in 1909. They walked together for miles and miles on the streets of London and into the country; they sat for hours and talked at the Restaurant des Gourmets; and sometimes Masefield visited Synge in his room at 4 Handel Street, Bloomsbury. Through Synge, Masefield came to understand the Irish people better and to realize the importance of writing about England and its folk ways. They last met shortly after the first London performance of Synge's *Playboy of the Western World* in 1907, and Masefield was fascinated by the way the play captured the tragic Irish spirit. Synge's play inspired the stage-struck Masefield to try his hand at playwriting and made him aware of the effectiveness of showing the rough as well as the tender aspects of life. Masefield accomplished this in his own way in his narrative poems *The Everlasting Mercy* and *The Widow in the Bye Street.*

Masefield's most lasting and most significant Irish relationship, however, was his marriage in 1903 to Constance de la Cherois-Crommelin of County Antrim in Northern Ireland. Constance was ten years older than he, and he found with her the contentment and the security that eluded so many of his contemporary writers. He lived happily and conventionally with his amiable, intelligent wife for fifty-seven years until she died in 1960. They had two children, Judith, born in 1905; Lewis, born in 1910.

Judith became a book illustrator; worked on several of her father's books; wrote successful children's books; and still lives and works in Midhurst, Sussex.[41] Lewis Crommelin Masefield, who studied at Rugby and Balliol College, Oxford, obtained the Classical education his father had been denied by circumstance; became a competent and talented journalist and novelist; but, to the enormous grief of his parents and his sister, was killed in 1942 at the age of thirty-two by German fire while serving with a British Army Red Cross Unit in North Africa. His father wrote a restrained but poignant biographical preface to Lewis's second and posthumously published novel, *The Passion Left Behind* (1947).[42]

John Masefield's first volume of poems was published in 1902, the year before his marriage. Called *Salt Water Ballads,* it was "written mainly in six exciting weeks." Although it "met with no welcome at the time,"[43] the poet recalled, it contained his "Sea-Fever," "Trade Winds," and "A Wanderer's Song," for which Masefield still remains famous. It is true that some of the poems in this and in *Ballads* (1903) were imitative, but others introduced the rough but bracing sailors' talk to readers who had hitherto been accustomed to the smooth-flowing lines of Tennyson or A.C. Swinburne. During this period, Masefield published two collections of sea stories, *A Mainsail Haul* (1905) and *A Tarpaulin Muster* (1907); two impressive novels, *Captain Margaret* (1908) and *Multitude and Solitude* (1909); two naval histories, *Sea Life in Nelson's Time* (1905) and *On the Spanish Main* (1906); his best plays, *The Tragedy of Nan* (1909), produced in 1908 by Granville Barker at the New Royalty Theatre in London, and *The Tragedy of Pompey the Great* (1910); *Ballads and Poems* (1910). In addition, he wrote numerous articles and reviews for periodicals. Masefield at this time considered himself to be, first of all, a playwright; but, after 1914, he abandoned this idea.[44]

His total volume of work from 1902 to 1910 is prodigious. In those few years he turned out more words, and good words too, than a great many of his fellow craftsmen produced in their entire lifetimes. He was not yet famous, but he was recognized by many as a serious and competent storyteller and poet. Most important of all for Masefield's family, he had achieved some financial security. In 1909, he moved his household from Greenwich[45] to the little village of Great Hampden, near Missenden in Buckinghamshire, some thirty miles from London.

III *Fame*

While walking near his new residence, Masefield made a new discovery about himself and his career:

In 1911, I first found what I could do. In this year, I began a way of writing in which I continued for several years. Towards the end of May in that most beautiful sunny year, it chanced that I went for a lonely evening walk in lonely country. I had walked for some miles. . . . As I thrust through the hedge which parted the beech-wood from a stretch of common land I said to myself, "Now I will write a poem about a blackguard who becomes converted." Immediately as I broke into the common land, the beginning of the poem floated up into my mind and I began to compose it. When I reached home I wrote down what I had composed, and wrote on with great eagerness until nearly midnight.[46]

Three weeks later Masefield had finished *The Everlasting Mercy*, the first of his long, great narratives. In narrative verse perhaps better than that of any Englishman since Chaucer, Masefield used unfashionable, crisp, brutal language and a simple, almost folk-like meter. His diction shocked the genteel Edwardian literary circles, but he endeared himself to the reading public, particularly those who were willing to read poetry, to enjoy the verse "novels" of one of their own—a man who had worked with his hands and who had not been to a university. *The Everlasting Mercy* (1911), *The Widow in the Bye Street* (1912), and *Dauber* (1913), all written within a two-year period, brought Masefield to the forefront of English poetry and led eventually to the Poet Laureateship in 1930.

When Masefield sent *The Everlasting Mercy* to the *English Review*, the editors, Austin Harrison and Norman Douglas, could not decide whether or not to publish the poem. For one, it was exceedingly long. Most disturbing, however, were the subject and the language, for expressions like "you closhy put" and "you bloody liar" were simply not seen in print. Nevertheless, the decision was to publish; and the issue provoked an uproar, one quite difficult to comprehend today. "It was even a bigger sensation than Kipling's *Barrack-Room Ballads*,"[47]—despite the fact that the editors had "compromised" by leaving blank all offending words. Although some readers and critics attacked this Grundyism, others blasted the *Review* for publishing such trash in the first place. As L. A. G. Strong indicates: .

> The poem fell roughly into the mill-pond of contemporary verse, and the rousing splash greatly enlivened the polite surface. Objection, parody, abuse, and praise spread in widening circles, leaving no inch untroubled. . ʒ. . Masefield had got himself talked about, not only by those who were interested in poetry, but by the far greater crowd of those who rush in angrily or derisively to damn what they do not understand. The foundations of his fame were laid: and, with characteristic vigour and courage he proceeded to build soundly upon them.[48]

At this time, Masefield was very much the *pater familius;* he was living in domestic harmony with Constance and their two children in their Great Hampden cottage. In 1912, when he was awarded the Edmond de Polignac Prize for *The Everlasting Mercy,* an enterprising American journalist, sensing that Masefield was fast becoming a major figure in British literature, made a pilgrimage to Great Hampden to meet the poet of the forecastle and the pub. When he was greeted by seven-year-old Judith at the front garden of the house, she took his letter of introduction to her father; and the American described the poet:

> Presently you hear footsteps; a man's voice tenderly addressing a child; and you are not surprised to see a fairly large, rather roughly dressed, but gentle looking person, a babe on his arm, appear in the doorway—it is Masefield, the Masefield your fancy has pictured, only more so—perhaps you hadn't counted on his hair being a bit red. But if you expected to find him human, you find him abnormally human. . . .
>
> A good, well-constructed head is Masefield's—attractively broad across the eyes; its lower jaw hints at strength without flaunting it. A tinge of gray in closely cropped hair adds not a little to its character; while the small mustache is an effective touch in the portrait because of its more pronounced red. The elusive eyes are a live hazel, bordering on gray; it is these that help to give the face, especially in three-quarter view, an indescribably gentle, soft and reflective aspect, that does not take away from its

masculine look, and only serves to give the countenance a certain quiet balance.[49]

In the course of the interview, Masefield expressed his particular admiration for Walt Whitman; for him, he was the "big voice" among American poets. But, not for the last time, Masefield acknowledged that "I owe everything to Yeats."[50]

As the journalist was being escorted to the garden gate at the conclusion of the interview Masefield suddenly stopped and exclaimed "Let me cut you some roses!" Then, "Having dispatched several of these with his penknife he deftly bound them together with a bit of twine, leaving a handy loop—reminiscent, perhaps, of his seafaring days—permitting their being carried without danger of being pricked by the thorns."[51] This act represented John Masefield, a man skilled with his hands, a giving man, a lover of the natural beauty of a rose, an Englishman.

Just prior to the outbreak of World War I, Masefield moved his family to an ancient house built by monks in the twelfth century at Lollingdon among the Berkshire downs.[52] Masefield was very happy there and then. He had achieved a large degree of literary success, he had found the emotional and economic security for which he had longed, and he anticipated a happy life as a literary gentleman with a country home and friends and agents to be visited in not-too-distant London. But August, 1914, destroyed his world as it destroyed that of hundreds of millions of human beings. Many of his friends like Rupert Brooke died, all emerged from the Götterdämmerung of the Edwardian world shaken and damaged; and the gentle grip of the Georgian poets on the helm of English poetry was brutally and forever smashed.

When Masefield's home was requisitioned by the cavalry as a billet, he watched with deep sadness the instruments of war parade by and the cavalry mounts watering at the moat.[53] Masefield, who befriended the troopers, was always fascinated as well as frightened by the military. The next time he met the men who had shared his home in 1914, they were without their brave chargers and their dress uniforms. Instead, they were in filthy khaki covered with lice; and, dripping sweat, they were seeking cover in shallow trenches while under heavy Turkish fire at Gallipoli. After that, Masefield's fascination for war turned, along with Europe's, to disgust and to horror.

As the war erupted into the undreamed of reality, Masefield wrote the poignant poem, "August, 1914," which was to several post-World War I critics the best poem that emerged from that period of conflict. In it, Masefield expresses his deep love for English earth and English traditions; but darkness sadly falls over both and "Over the grasses of the ancient / Rutted this morning by the passing guns." Although hardly a jingoist, and certainly not in sympathy with Rudyard Kipling's imperialistic values, Masefield felt not only that the Allied cause was just but that the few influential pacifists like Bertrand Russell and George Bernard Shaw were wrong. Masefield was never able either during or after both world wars to effect a dehumanizing of the Germans into "Hun" or "Boche," no matter how close death struck to him. There was just too much humanity in Masefield for such blind, collective judgments.

When he tried to enlist, he could not be accepted for combat duty because his youthful illnesses had taken too great a toll. Since his early interest in medicine had not entirely waned, he took service with the British Red Cross, sailing to France late in 1914.[54] In 1915, the great Dardanelles disaster occurred; and the ill-fated Gallipoli campaign found the former sailor commanding a picket boat that towed barges of wounded out from the blood-soaked beaches to the waiting destroyers. The sickness rate at Gallipoli was devastating; and the thirty-seven-year-old writer, who had been piloting his boat and tending the wounded from dawn to dusk seven days a week, became ill with fever and had to be evacuated home with the soldiers.

In January, 1916, as soon as Masefield was well enough, he sailed for America to lecture on behalf of the British war effort and the Red Cross. The American audiences, while generally quite sympathetic, were nevertheless critical of the Dardanelles campaign and questioned its wisdom and purpose. Masefield wrote:

People asked me why that attempt had been made, why it had been made in that particular manner, why other courses had not been taken, why this had been done and that either neglected or forgotten, and whether a little more persistence, here or there, would not have given us the victory.

These questions were often followed by criticism of various kinds, some of it plainly suggested by our enemies, some of it shrewd, and some the honest opinion of men and women happily ignorant of modern war. I answered questions and criticism as best I could, but in the next town they were repeated to me, and in the town beyond reiterated, until I felt the need of a leaflet printed for distribution, giving my views of the matter.[55]

But Masefield's leaflet was not enough; he had to prove that, although Gallipoli was a strategic failure, it was sound in concept and represented a great triumph for the human spirit, like the long defense of Troy. As a result of such a need, Masefield settled in at Lollingdon, began to write *Gallipoli*, and completed that fine prose work in three months. After he had also published a new verse collection, *Lollingdon Downs* (1917), he returned to the field hospitals in France. There he worked on his second war study, *The Old Front Line* (1917), was commissioned a lieutenant in the British Expeditionary Force, and was offered (but refused) a knighthood for his varied war services.[56]

Masefield returned to the United States at the behest of the British government in January, 1918, to generate additional American aid, cooperation, and enthusiasm for the war effort. During this visit of nearly seven months, he spoke everywhere and at every opportunity as the military situation grew darker for the Allies on the Western Front. That his good humor and his love of adventure did not desert him during those hectic and emotionally difficult days is indicated by his recollection of his first flying experience:

I was asked to a big camp to speak at a mess. So I went and spoke at the camp, which is one of the biggest aviation camps in the world. Last July it was a vast flat plain, covered with scrub, which they call mezquite and chaparral. . . . Now it is an immense and splendid city, humming with life and machines, with great roads and theatres and irrigations, and a vast populace of mechanics. And there I met an airman, who would take no denial, but that I should come up with him, as it was a good day for flying.

So I put on a leather coat and leather cap and goggles and I saw my machine on the ground. . . . Then I climbed into my seat and was strapped in, and was told not to monkey with the machinery, which was quite the last thing I ever thought of doing. Then they turned her round, head to wind, and my driver got in, and after some preliminaries they touched her off.

For the first hundred yards or so, it was just like being in a motor car, but as we ran along the ground the thing became alive, like a very eager, wonderful, trembling horse that was on her mettle and was going at a big leap, and I felt all her excitement, and wanted to pat her on her neck and give her a lump of sugar, and her cylinders became louder and louder, and her rush more wonderful, and then suddenly we were off the ground and slowly rising, and no longer conscious of motion, except that there was a roaring gale in one's face, and a great roar from the propeller. Then, looking down, I saw the ground like a vast chess-board, and people like dots, and then we began to tilt in great circles as we climbed, and that was a deep emotion, but still I was far less conscious of flying than I have been at sea in a sailing ship when working aloft.

. . . .

My man stopped the engines, and we floated there in utter silence but for the wind, and in a stillness and steadiness so strange that we could not tell we were moving; so then we talked for half a minute, and then he touched her off again, and we went for a cruise.

Coming down was so gradual that it did not rouse much emotion, and the actual landing, which I had expected to be a bump, was not really more than a car would make in crossing a rut in a road; but when one got out, one felt a little odd. Anyhow, the queerness only lasted about thirty seconds, and the main impression left one of great interest and beauty and unreality, not exactly of pleasant interest, nor of human beauty, but it was a new thing, and I was glad to have done it—though I felt that it belonged to this generation, and not to mine.[57]

The Allied military crisis passed; and, with the fresh American troops aiding in the counter offensive, victory for the Allies grew more certain daily. In the summer of 1918, Masefield returned to England to work on *The War and the Future* (1918), which he dedicated to his American friend Thomas William Lamont, and on *The Battle of the Somme* (1919), which was Masefield's last study of World War I. Although a tidal flood of war memoirs, histories, apologies, novels, poems, and films inundated the world, the poet who had made a religion of beauty in a pre-Raphaelite way and who had loved folk ways and crafts, had no more stomach for, or illusions about, war. Furthermore, he suspected that many readers also felt the same way. To the surprise of many critics and to the disappointment of others, Masefield's next major work was the narrative poem *Reynard the Fox* (1919).

Like so many war-weary people, Masefield wanted to be with his family again in a home that provided some refuge from the problems of the day and from the nightmares of yesterday. With this end in mind and in preparation for his postwar work, Masefield moved Constance and their children to a large house "Hill Crest" at Boar's Hill near Oxford in 1917. From this home, which became something of a literary Mecca for a brief time, Masefield, like Matthew Arnold's Scholar-Gypsy, could see the distant spires of Oxford. Indeed, Masefield may have yearned for peaceful country life as well as for the intellectual stimulation that a great university could provide.

A badly wounded war hero and a fledgeling writer who had left Oxford undergraduate life to join the British forces and who, as a married student, returned to his studies in 1920, asked Masefield, whom he had met on leave in 1917, to help him with his housing problem. The young writer, who had a case of hero-worship for the older sea poet, was Robert Graves; and he recalled after Masefield's death that:

Masefield generously rented me a cottage at the bottom of his Boar's Hill garden. I remember his shy morning smile and hello, when I used to trudge by his garden workshed half hidden among gorse trees; he was, as often as not, idly engrossed in a favorite foc'sle occupation: carving and rigging model sailing ships.

I grew greatly attached to John Masefield, as also did our neighbour, the poet Edmund Blunden, another young battle-shocked ex-officer, now Professor of Poetry at Oxford. Though members of a rebellious new generation, we declined to ally ourselves poetically with the Franco-American modernists—the Sitwells, Eliot, Pound, H. D. Flint, Read and the rest. We remained as obstinately rooted in the early English tradition as Masefield himself, who was Chaucer's man.[58]

The years at Boar's Hill were perhaps Masefield's happiest. His children grew to maturity, his health firmed, poetry and prose cascaded from his hand, honors were rained upon him, and ultimately the Laureateship was offered him. Here too, he was able to satisfy, in part, his old love for the theater. His plays had really not been commercial successes, and he slowly came to realize that he was not a dramatist. Instead of writing for the London stage, he decided to establish his own private theater at Boar's Hill; he built a large music room in the garden where his plays, some classics, and some works of unknown moderns were produced; and his friends like Sir Julian and Juliette Huxley, as well as his daughter Judith and Oxford dons and undergraduates, played various roles. Many a literary light, including Mr. and Mrs. George Bernard Shaw, made their way up to Oxford for an evening with John Masefield and the drama.[59]

In 1920, Masefield published another successful narrative poem, *Right Royal*, and, in 1921, *King Cole*, a verse narrative, to which Judith Masefield contributed drawings. Nonetheless, Masefield's ever-growing interest in, and love for, storytelling caused him to reconsider the novel as a means of expression. Masefield's first novel, *Captain Margaret* (1908) had not been a great success; and his boys' books like *Martin Hyde: The Duke's Messenger* (1910), and *Jim Davis* (1911), while well received, had been neither satisfying nor serious enough for the writer. He had long admired Joseph Conrad's ability to relate in a most profound way the trials of men and the ways of the sea. As a result, Masefield began a series of novels about the Central American coast and about young men in crisis at sea.

Sard Harker (1924), the first novel about a young Englishman's adventure in the mythological Central American republic of Santa Barbara, was well received by critics who compared Masefield to Tobias Smollett, Thomas Hardy, and Conrad. The comparisons were generous; the story, if not profound, was exciting and the characters believable; but Masefield's Central American novels and his English countryside novels pale in comparison to those of Conrad or Hardy. Masefield's *ODTAA* (1926), which soon followed, was another Central American work. He continued to produce other forms of literature: the dramas *The Trial of Jesus* (1925) and *Tristan and Isolt* (1927); the poetry collections *Midsummer Night* (1928) and *Minnie Maylow's Story* (1931); his critical studies of *William Shakespeare* (1925) and of *Chaucer* (1931); and his history of his great ship-symbol, *The Wanderer of Liverpool* (1930). However, his major interest at this period in his life was the novel.

Masefield's first important work of fiction dealing with English country life was *The Hawbucks* (1929), which was fairly well received. From 1933 through 1935, Masefield published his three best novels: *The Bird of Dawning* (1933) and *Victorious Troy: or The Hurrying Angel* (1935), superb tales of young men against the sea are reminiscent of Conrad's *Typhoon;* while *The Taking of the Gry* (1934) is Masefield's last and best Central American novel. Although other novels followed, Masefield's talent as a prose storyteller became somewhat diluted, perhaps due to the demands of the poet laureate role.

IV   *The Laureateship*

When Poet Laureate Robert Bridges died on April 21, 1930, the position of poet laureate had great prestige; for many still associated the laureateship with Wordsworth and Tennyson who had been enormously popular as well as first-class poets. Bridges had been considered quite satisfactory, and only Alfred Austin's laureateship from 1896 - 1913 had detracted from the luster of the appointment. The unofficial candidates for the replacement of Bridges included Rudyard Kipling (who probably would have received the appointment if the Prime Minister at the time had not been the Laborite, Ramsay MacDonald), G. K. Chesterton, W. W. Gibson, A. E. Housman, Walter de la Mare, and Alfred Noyes. Yeats, despite great critical support, was really not to be considered since he was an Irish senator and thus a part of the Dublin government.

The decision came quickly; some said too quickly. MacDonald recommended Masefield to King George V. His Majesty was himself an old sailor who had trained in windjammers and who loved Masefield's sea ballads. On May 9, 1930, an official communiqué announced: "The King has been graciously pleased to appoint John Masefield, Esq., D. Litt., to be Poet Laureate in ordinary to his Majesty in the room of Robert Bridges, Esq., O.M., D. Litt., M.A., deceased." The appointment was acclaimed by the general public both in Great Britain and America; but although professional critics were generally favorable, some disappointed supporters of other candidates expressed their dissent. Writers in *The Nation, Publishers' Weekly, The Christian Century, The Canadian Forum* all reacted favorably to Masefield's appointment. Of American publications, only *The Saturday Review of Literature* expressed some hesitation. A. E. Housman, George Bernard Shaw, John Drinkwater, G. K. Chesterton, J. B. Priestly, John Galsworthy, and even Edith Sitwell offered affirmative statements about Masefield's suitability and qualifications.

Masefield, who accepted the great honor with his customary sincere humility, stated that it was not his intention to change his methods or his subjects—nor did he intend to crank out occasional poems upon royal occasions or national events. For four years Masefield maintained his intentions; but, after 1934, he began to write "official" verse for the London *Times*, and published twenty-two poems in that paper between 1934 and 1950. Not coincidentally, Masefield's decline as a creative writer dates from the beginning of his serious assumption of Laureate duties. The decade prior to World War II was filled with honors, degrees, prestigious lectures, trips showing the cultural flag, and succeedingly weaker and weaker collections of verse and works of fiction in which the public man seemed to have devoured the creative soul. Although Masefield refused knighthood on several occasions, he did accept the coveted Order of Merit in 1935, as Bridges and Henry James had before him, and as T. S. Eliot did later.

There were family moves too. The Masefields left Boar's Hill in 1932 for Pinbury Park, Cirencester, Gloucestershire. They had a splendid house with a long driveway lined with two magnificent rows of walnut trees that were said to have been planted with nuts taken from Napoleon's table at Elba.[60] In 1938, they moved again but for the last time to the Burcote Brook House at Abingdon, Berkshire, near Oxford. In his last anchorage, the old sailor could gaze out of his living room to the narrow reaches of the upper Thames, watch the flowing waters that led down to the city, and speculate about the ships and the eternal sea.[61]

As Masefield reached his sixties, his hope for a quiet, dignified old age with Constance and for visits from his children and perhaps grandchildren was shattered by the global disaster of World War II when his beloved England was in even greater danger in 1939 from the German enemy than it was in 1914. The fall of France brought despair to Masefield as it did to all his countrymen, but the successful evacuation of over three-hundred-thousand men of the British Expeditionary Force from Dunkirk by the Royal Navy and by the seamen and yachtsmen of Britain so lifted Masefield's spirits that he wrote his "*Gallipoli*" of the 1939-1945 war: *The Nine Days Wonder* (1941). The book is a stirring prose account of the evacuation, Operation Dynamo, from May 26 through June 3, 1940; and concludes with poems of thanks and praise for the young men of Britain.

Once more the grey-haired Masefield worked for the Allied cause. He made broadcasts and lectured in hospitals. When the Americans entered the war, Masefield visited United States Army camps in England and read his poetry before large and small groups. Because of Masefield's advancing years and because of the constant news of death and destruction as yet another generation of young men were carted out as grist for the mill of the war god,

Masefield turned back in his thoughts and in his writing to his early years; and a group of autobiographical poems and prose works flowed from his unfaltering pen. In 1940, just after his beloved mentor had died, Masefield paid his homage to the great Irish poet in *Some Memories of W. B. Yeats.*

Then, at sixty-two, when his storytelling and narrative powers found a new outlet in autobiography, Masefield chose not to write a sweeping history of his own life but to take select short periods such as his tour aboard the *Conway* and his Yonkers experience and probe them for their artistic and philosophical impact. In 1941, he wrote *In the Mill,* his recollections of his life in the Yonkers carpet factory and one of Masefield's most interesting and best written prose works.

Somewhat less successfully, and in imitation of Wordsworth's *The Prelude,* Masefield attempted to treat his early childhood in verse through *Wonderings. Between One and Six Years* (1943). *New Chum* (1944), the story of his first term as an apprentice aboard the *Conway,* picked up the verve of *In the Mill* to the delight of his readers young and old. A literary autobiographical work, *So Long to Learn* (1952), and *Grace Before Ploughing* (1966) proved obtuse, strained, and disappointing to readers attempting to learn facts about Masefield's life.

V   *The End of Wandering*

Constance died on February 18, 1960; Judith cared for her father; but Masefield began to fail. In late 1966, when he developed gangrene in an ankle, his attending physicians wished to amputate the foot; but Masefield refused. The weeks dragged by; the pain was excruciating; and Masefield, who had once more refused an operation, reconciled himself to death. His last days were spent happily with Judith in reminiscence and farewell. On May 12, 1967, just before his eighty-ninth birthday the lean, tired, old storyteller died in the Burcote Brook house.[62] At a memorial service held on June 20, 1967, a small urn with Masefield's ashes was interred in the Poet's Corner of Westminster Abbey next to Robert Browning. The marker now reads: "John Masefield, O.M. 1878-1967." Writing about John Masefield before he died, Muriel Spark said:

he does not think of himself mainly as a poet, as a novelist, a Poet Laureate, as a grand old man of letters, or anything of the sort. He seems to count it his first vocation to be a human being with an infinite curiosity about the activities of other human beings. Few living poets share with him this unselfconscious attitude. The enactment of life appears to be his first interest, both in himself and in others. As he is a writer, he defines; as he is a poet, he seeks the essential features of life; but first of all he is a participant in life.[63]

John Masefield was a human being and a literary artist who pulled a long, deep drink from the cup of life. For his experience was everything and he had indeed slaked his thirst.

CHAPTER 2

Early Verse

M ASEFIELD, who was by no means a child prodigy, was twenty four when his first book was published. But in the period between the publication of *Salt Water Ballads* in 1902 and *The Everlasting Mercy* in 1911 Masefield served a journeymanship to professional writing that was as intense, varied, and successful as that any writer ever experienced. Three books of poetry, four novels, two collections of stories, two historical works, two play collections, and assorted miscellaneous works including nearly two hundred book reviews tumbled from his smoking pen; but his best and most long-lived product was his verse. Although critics found them sometimes imitative, sometimes flawed, and not very profound, the early poems of Masefield eventually won their way to the hearts of English speakers the world over; in fact, many of his ballads and short lyrics are today among the most loved and most remembered pieces that survived the Edwardian Age.

I *Salt Water Poems and Ballads*

The small first book of 1902 that John Masefield cast out to the world on a young author's chain of hopes was *Salt Water Ballads;* it made almost no splash although "Sea-Fever," with its nostalgic cry for a simpler life and the joy of the elements, has become famous; and its lines are often quoted: "I must down to the seas again, to the lonely sea and the sky, / And all I ask is a tall ship and a star to steer her by. . . ." The opening poem, "A Consecration," is noble and fitting for a writer who had risen from the ranks; for his song is "Not of the princes and prelates with periwigged charioteers / Riding triumphantly laurelled to lap the fat of the years,— / Rather the scorned—the rejected—the men hemmed in with the spears. . . ." And, of course, Masefield interjects his own early life at sea:

42

> The sailor, the stoker of steamers, the man with the clout,
> The chantyman bent at the halliards putting a tune to the shout,
> The drowsy man at the wheel and the tired lookout.
>
> . . . .
>
> Of these shall my songs be fashioned, my tales be told.

Masefield's stylistic thrust in *Salt Water Ballads* is realistic but, paradoxically, the effect is romantic. The collection of sea poems is so filled with esoteric seaman's language that it was published with a glossary of nautical terms. The sailors' lingo was used, of course, for its realism. However, although the collection of ballads supposedly represented stories recited by seafaring men, the ritualistic language, the procedures of seamen, the exotic settings, and the melodramatic subjects worked against realism even in Edwardian days. Today, because of the disappearance of commercial sail shipping, a process that had begun even before Masefield went to sea, the sea poems are about as "realistic" as the medieval "Seafarer" or "Wanderer."

In fact, the ultimate invocation of *Salt Water Ballads* and Masefield's immediately succeeding work *Ballads* (1903), books that are considered together, is that of a communal mythology of sailors. The collections are a kind of Testament or Talmud that contain mythological lore, advice to young sailors, near-contemporary legends, health tips, and other manual-like information. In "Fever Ship," the seamen are hard and calloused but also exceedingly nostalgic and sentimental:

> There'll be no weepin' gells ashore when *our* ship sails
> Nor no crews cheerin' us, standin' at the rails,
> 'N' no Blue Peter a-foul the royal stay.
> For we've the Yellow Fever—Harry died to-day—
> It's cruel when a fo'c's'le gets the fever!

Nevertheless, the poems of *Salt Water Ballads* and *Ballads* have a richness, a youthful vitality, and lines that contain an almost tropical sense of intense color, as in "Bill"—When the rising moon was a copper disc and the sea was a strip of steel, / We dumped him down to the swaying weeds ten fathom beneath the keel"—or as in "The Turning of the Tide": "An' dreaming down below there in the tangled greens an' blues, / Where the sunlight shudders golden round about. . . ."

The poems in *Salt Water Ballads* are presented as yarns actually spoken by sailor *personae*. In *Ballads*, the pieces are of greater variety; there are London poems, love sonnets and songs as well as first-person ballads and short sea verse like the memorable "Cargoes," which celebrates the history of shipping from the "Quinquireme of Nineveh from distant Orphir" through a Spanish galleon down to a "Dirty British coaster" of modern times. Whereas *Salt Water Ballads* is a unified selected group of poems forming a true book in its attempt to effect a mood and to depict a way of life, *Ballads* is a compendium in which the poet selected from his experiments a variety of successful pieces. A more typical poetry collection, it lacks a central theme or an architectonic device.

Masefield, like Kipling in *Barrack Room Ballads*, seems to have decided from the beginning to shock the conservative reading public of his time by a calculated use of language and of image usually not then considered publishable.[1] He remembered this eye-opening possibility and later applied it with enormous success in the poem that made him a national figure, *The Everlasting Mercy*. Expressions like "bloody" or "dirty Dago lad" were simply unseen in polite print and were not heard in polite conversation, but Masefield relished the effect of passages like the following one from "Sing a Song o' Shipwreck":

> " 'N' then the stooard goes dotty 'n' puts a tune to his lip,
> 'N' moans about Love like a dern old hen wi' the pip—
> (I sets no store upon stooards—they aint no use on a ship).
> " 'N' 'mother,' the looney cackles, 'come 'n' put Willy to bed!'
> So I says 'Dry up, or I'll fetch you a crack o' the head';
> 'The kettle's a-bilin',' he answers, ' 'n' I'll go butter the bread.'

or the opening stanza of "Cape Horn Gospel I":

> "I was in a hooker once," said Karlssen,
> "And Bill, as was a seaman, died,
> So we lashed him in an old tarpaulin
> And tumbled him across the side;
> And the fun of it was that all his gear was
> Divided up among the crew
> Before that blushing human error,
> Our crawling little captain, knew.

and the first two stanzas of "Cape Horn Gospel II":

Jake was a dirty Dago lad, an' he gave the skipper chin,
An' the skipper up an' took him a crack with an iron belaying-pin
Which stiffened him out a rusty corp, as pretty as you could wish,
An' then we shovelled him up in a sack an' dumped him to the fish.
    That was jest after we'd got sail on her.
'Josey slipped from the tops'l-yard an' bust his bloody back
(Which comed from playing the giddy goat an' leavin' go the jack);
We lashed his chips in clouts of sail an' ballasted him with stones,
"The Lord hath taken away," we says, an' we give him to Davy Jones.
    An' that was afore we were up with the Line.

Masefield was trying, and ultimately succeeded for a little while, to bring serious "poetry down to the plain reader in the street."[2] No one later lamented more than Masefield the growing alienation of the poet from the public in the post-World War I era. For Masefield, poetry was an auxiliary to life, an aid in enduring, a delight, and a means to an end such as the good life. Poetry was not to be an end unto itself for the young Masefield, and it never became one. He makes this point clear in "Spunyarn": "I have travelled on land and sea, and all that I have found / Are these poor songs to brace the arms that help the winches round."

The short poem "Beauty" is an example of the emerging esthetics of Masefield—a cult of beauty worship based on the anthropomorphizing and then the deifying of man-made objects like ships—and of the various influences that were working on the young poet because of his eclectic reading:

I have seen dawn and sunset on moors and windy hills
Coming in solemn beauty like slow old tunes of Spain:
I have seen the lady April bringing the daffodils,
Bringing the springing grass and the soft warm April rain.
I have heard the song of the blossoms and the old chant of the sea,
And seen strange lands from under the arched white sails of ships;
But the loveliest things of beauty God ever has showed to me,
Are her voice, and her hair, and eyes, and the dear red curve of her lips.

The romantic "I" opens the poem, and the pedestrian "solemn beauty" is invoked by a simile probably included only because "Spain" and "rain" rhyme. Chaucer's "shoures soote" of April have also engendered Masefield's flowers. The "song of the blossoms and the old chant of the sea" represents the two major and entwining subject areas in Masefield's work: the English countryside and the sea. The ship—crafted, functional, moving, distant, a thing of the land exiled to a life and a death in another element—appears in the poem's best image as a beauty symbol; and strange lands are seen "from under the arched white sails of ships." This framed, composed, evocative image is almost unbelievably driven out of mind by the prosaic "loveliest things of beauty." When the poem then climaxes with some of Masefield's few references to a woman's anatomy, he discreetly keeps above the shoulders but establishes the ultimate ideal for beauty, the female, for whom the ship becomes the surrogate symbol in much of the remainder of the poet's work.

There is much adolescent brooding on twilight and death in these early poems. The reader is exhorted to "Laugh till the game is played," and the female addressee of "June Twilight" is asked: "Love, can this beauty in our hearts end?" Masefield soon left brooding on death, but the time of twilight was "always significant for Masefield—the hour of remembrance, the hour of the ending quest."[3] In the second and last stanza of "Twilight," the softness, gentleness, and sincerity of the verse transcend the sentimentality of the thought and of the juvenile theology:

> I think of the friends who are dead, who were dear long ago in the past,
> Beautiful friends who are dead, though I know that death cannot last;
> Friends with the beautiful eyes that the dust has defiled,
> Beautiful souls who were gentle when I was a child.

The lovely Pre-Raphaelite moments—gentle, delicate and sad—in these first lyrics are many. In "The Harper's Song" the musical instrument and the bard (Masefield) bring forth

> The old cunning wakened from the wires
> The old sorrows and the old desires.
>
> Dead Kings in long forgotten lands,
>   And all dead beauteous women; some
>   Whose pride imperial hath become
> Old armour rusting in the sands
> And shards of iron in dusty hands,
>
> Have heard my lyre's soft rise and fall
>   Go trembling down the paven ways,
>   Till every heart was all ablaze—
> Hasty each foot—to obey the call
> To triumph or to funeral.

Unlike the ballads of the early collections, the lyrics speak of the poet's contribution: the Harper moves men to thoughts of past beauty and grandeur; he fires their hearts for living and for dying. Most of all, it is beauty which the poet seeks and serves: he is troubadour to an abstract queen. As in "Roadways," Masefield's journey will be "In quest of that one beauty / God put me here to find."

Nonetheless, the best of Masefield's early poetry are the sea stories, for they contain the uniqueness which is essential to every significant poet. They have the power and, to use an infrequent term in criticism, the energy to sustain a poetic imagination through the long pull of a life in the arts. And they contain in form and language the germs of Masefield's later success as England's possibly last great narrative poet.

II *First Narratives*

Despite an overlay of Yeatsian nostalgia—and what sensitive young poet could ignore the influence of the greatest English language poet of the twentieth century?—Masefield's early ballads are tough, salty, and highly communicative of a life that was cruel, dangerous, crude, painful, and sometimes unbelievably terrible. The nostalgia is for the passing of such a life and that is where the weakness of the ballads lies. For windjammer life was dying even before Masefield went to sea and his longing for the seaman's fight against nature came years after he himself had given up that struggle.

Some of these first ballads particularly prefigure Masefield's later great narratives. The style and emphasis on story line in *The Everlasting Mercy, Reynard the Fox*, and others, stem from such shorter narrations as "The Yarn of the Loch Achray." In this ballad, Masefield tells the story of the wreck of the clipper ship *Loch Achray* with all hands lost, while their wives and sweethearts wait in the rain for their loved ones who will never return. Masefield is beginning to develop the ability to paint a scene dramatically:

> Then a fierce squall struck the *Loch Achray*
> And bowed her down to her water-way;
> Her main-shrouds gave and her forestay,
> And a green sea carried her wheel away;

Even Masefield's characterization, which always lags in the early narrative ballads, is on the upswing:

The old man said, "I mean to hang on
Till her canvas busts, or her sticks are gone"—
Which the blushing looney did, till at last
Overboard went her mizzen-mast.

In "Sing a Song o' Shipwreck," a tough old sailor who survives a shipwreck has a corpse for a companion as he clings to the keel of a capsized whaleboat. "One of the Bo'sun's Yarns," the longest of the early narrative ballads, has some one hundred twelve alternating lines of iambic tetrameter and iambic trimeter. Like the Ancient Mariner who tells his tale to the wedding guest, one sailor is telling a yarn as it was told to him by another who drank him out of his wages in the process. The internal storyteller had shipped out of Hull on a tramp named the *Esmeralda* which was rammed by a steamer one night in a fog. The tough old mate, whom all hands hated, bullies some of the seamen into making a raft just before the *Esmeralda's* boilers blow. The mate's brutality and his underlying humanity are both necessary for survival in a sea disaster, and it is primarily through his efforts that seven men survive the wreck of the *Esmeralda*. The poem turns on character, for intelligence and toughness mixed with integrity, no matter how rough the mold of the man, permit the survival of the body and the triumph of the spirit in the face of catastrophe:

"Then the mate came dancin' on to the scene, 'n' he says, 'Now quit yer chin,
Or I'll smash yer skulls, so help me James, 'n' let some wisdom in.
Ye dodderin' scum o' the slums,' he says, 'are ye drunk or blazin' daft?
If ye wish to save yer sickly hides, ye'd best contrive a raft.'

"So he spoke us fair and turned us to, 'n' we wrought wi' tooth and nail
Wi' scantling, casks, 'n' coops 'n ropes, 'n' boiler-plates 'n' sail,
'N' all the while it were dark 'n' cold 'n' dirty as it could be,
'N' she was soggy 'n' settlin' down to a berth beneath the sea.

Masefield was developing a rough-sounding, declarative style that would serve him well; he was experimenting successfully; his ideas, thoughts, and values were driving their way through the verse forms and the postures with which he worked. His early language managed to transcend the late Romantic manner of most of his contemporaries, and the catalyst that permitted this transcendence was the idiom of the sailor's world. Masefield presented situations that were fresh to the reading public of his time, and he continued to do so for another thirty years. Then, when seemingly at the height of his mature powers, he fell away from this understanding and declined as a poet.

In *Salt Water Ballads* and in *Ballads and Poems*, Masefield successfully blended common speech and common experience, albeit that of sailors, with the requirements of poetry which, after all, is a highly organized and artificial use of language. In *The Everlasting Mercy* and in the other great narratives, Masefield did the same for the language and experience of the provincial landsman. This juxtaposing of the common vernacular and the traditional organization of poetical language is, as Muriel Spark observes, "a technique we are used to finding in modern poetry, but we should not forget that Mr. Masefield was a pioneer exponent of it in the present century."[4] Amy Lowell also recognized the transitional nature of Masefield's early poetry as if he were the very embodiment of the evolving art of the early twentieth century. His technique, in particular his storytelling in verse, might, she thought, look back "to an older, vanished England. Yet also, he is very modern, he is modern man in his psychological reactions, he is modern man in his pity, his stern resolve to face life's cruelty and bitterness with no comforting plaster of lies spread upon it."[5]

CHAPTER 3

The Narratives

JOHN Masefield thought of himself ultimately as a storyteller. Although he wrote novels—some strong, some indifferent—and plays that were mostly contrived, he found in narrative verse the best means to express the art of storytelling. He made his reputation as a narrative poet, but he lost it as his ability to write narratives waned and as public taste for that old-fashioned genre died. "He was the last, or almost the last, major narrative poet using English. Chaucer, in effect, inaugurated this tradition. Chaucer was Masefield's master—though he was also to learn of others."[1]

Masefield wrote eight major narratives: *The Everlasting Mercy* (1911), *The Widow in the Bye Street* (1912), *Dauber* (1913), *The Daffodil Fields* (1913), *Reynard the Fox* (1919), *Enslaved* (1920), *Right Royal* (1920), and *King Cole* (1921). Of his six narratives set in the English countryside—*The Everlasting Mercy, The Widow in the Bye Street, The Daffodil Fields, Reynard the Fox, Right Royal,* and *King Cole*—the first two are clearly placed in the poet's home town of Ledbury and in his home shire of Herefordshire. In these poems and in certain of the novels, Masefield attempts to assign to the land the thematic and symbolic proportions that were more successfully attained by Thomas Hardy for his Wessex. *Dauber* is a sea poem that contains a long flashback to England, and *Enslaved* is set in North Africa.

One important fact about the art of the narrative poem in general as well as Masefield's narrative art in particular must be made since the modern reader of poetry is used to and expects highly concentrated, economical, and heavily imagistic language designed to be read silently from the printed page. Since the narrative poem has traditionally been written to be read aloud and heard, it must set a scene and convey motion by direct statement. Unlike the verse play, the verse narrative is accompanied neither with the visualization of

50

an actor nor a set. Furthermore, the plot is the poem's major architectonic device and the setting comes next. Lastly and perhaps most important to the understanding of the verse narrative is the fact that the density of the poem may only be that which is graspable during its first and single hearing. The reader cannot stop the narrator and ask him to say a stanza again, but the reader can go back again and again to a difficult passage in a printed non-narrative poem.

A particularly individual quality of Masefield's narratives, and especially of *The Everlasting Mercy, The Widow in the Bye Street, Right Royal* and *Reynard the Fox.* is the eyewitness-like account of the significant action of the tale. The reader is made to feel that he is a spectator at the boxing match and a pursuer in the chase in *The Everlasting Mercy;* that he is in the stands at the horserace in *Right Royal;* that he is a newsreel or television camera following Reynard as he leaps for his life. In fact, the reader of such narrative verse almost seems to interview the near-victim and to ask for his reactions, plans, and feelings. As Muriel Spark points out, Masefield seems almost to anticipate the contemporary television or radio commentator who is describing a sports event or, more particularly, a state occasion such as the funeral of a President.[2]

Masefield may have inadvertently summarized his personal goals for his narrative verse in his study of Chaucer. He states that England's first great poet's "concern was to give Life, to strip his characters and situations down to their Realities, and to make his statement of them intense and living, to burn away and hammer out everything that was not in character and in keeping, to make one see the place and to see and hear the people . . . poetry only can give this concentrated intensity. . . ."[3] In this statement, Masefield seems to be indicating his special preference for the telling of tales in verse rather than in prose. Although poetry was the ultimate anvil for the art of language, Masefield was frequently successful in establishing place and character through the evocative power of poetry.

In considering Chaucer's art in relation to his time, Masefield's view in the following, illuminating passage could equally describe himself and express also the relationship of his own art to the first half of the twentieth century:

Chaucer was born into an age as greedy of tales as this age. He was born with a rare aptness for the telling of tales, and with a greedy fondness for

them. A story and leave to tell a story were what he most wanted from life.
To read and to tell stories made up that Law of his Being, which men of
genius obey.

The problems: what made a tellable tale for his mood at the time: and
how to tell the tale chosen were the main concerns of his art. All through
his life, his leisure was given to the study of stories and to attempts to tell
them.

Some people to-day wonder why he did not tell the tales in prose: well,
sometimes he did; and those who read his tales in prose will perhaps be
thankful that it was not his usual practice.[4]

Masefield, from his days on the *Conway*, had the aptness and
fondness for stories; but finding plots and selecting literary methods
for telling his stories were his main artistic pursuits as a writer of
verse narratives as well as of novels and plays. He personally loved
to read stories and to tell them to his live audiences. And, unlike
just about every major British or American poet who followed him,
Masefield wrote his long verse narratives with his audience clearly
conceptualized. This new work of his was not "art for art's sake"
nor was it poetry written for the esoteric appreciation of other poets
and of scholar-critics. Masefield's was a people's poetry written for
the pleasure and the edification of the mass English-speaking
audience.

Significantly, Masefield turned to the long narrative, beginning
with *The Everlasting Mercy* in 1911, after he had written and
published his best plays, *The Tragedy of Nan* (1909) and *The
Tragedy of Pompey the Great* (1910). His experience as a writer of
dramatic verse also implanted the need to communicate with a live,
specific audience in his poetry and this understanding carried over
into the verse narratives. Furthermore, Masefield published his
study of *Shakespeare* (1911) just as he was submitting *The
Everlasting Mercy* to the *English Review*. Since he was writing the
critical study and the poem at the same time, his deep reading and
his critical evaluation of Shakespeare's plays emphasized the
presence of the audience in the work of public poetry. One must
greatly admire Masefield's sheer courage in attempting to speak to
the mass audience of English readers, for such art could only bring
down upon him the scorn of arrogant, elitist, undemocratic critics.
And Masefield must have known it would happen.

Masefield's ability as a writer of narrative verse peaked in the
1920s and the 1930s contiguous with the rise of the literary dic-
tatorship of T. S. Eliot and his followers. As Poet Laureate,

Masefield was an obvious target; and, by World War II, his reputation as a poet had been destroyed partly through the attack of the modernists but primarily through the changing practices and values of modern poetry. The verse narrative was defunct, even though *Prufrock* (1915) and *The Wasteland* (1922) have distinct narrative elements and might have led poetry into new forms of narrative instead of toward an esoteric lyricism.

Finally, if any reader of poetry believes that one allowable function of verse is the telling of a story—as did Chaucer, Sidney, Shakespeare, Milton, Pope, Wordsworth, Coleridge, Shelley, Byron, Keats, Tennyson, and Browning—then he must allow the author of *The Everlasting Mercy* and *Reynard the Fox* his place in the pantheon of English poets, for Masefield's verse narratives are highly crafted, superb works of art and possibly the last of their kind that the world of English language poetry may ever see.

I   *The Everlasting Mercy*

No reader today can easily envision the shock with which the literary public received *The Everlasting Mercy* nor can he comprehend the reason for the poem's sensational reception. Clearly, it seemed something very new; but, of course, narrative poems were not new, nor were they at all uncommon in 1911. The raw, unbridled energy and pace of the poem were new; the tough, direct street language was new; and the bold, unabashed thrust of moral theme and character of the poem was as excitingly contemporary as a Salvation Army street-corner sermon. *The Everlasting Mercy* swept readers along on a tidal wave of emotion. Like an evangelist's pitch, it was for the heart and the gut first; for the mind, only afterwards.

The Everlasting Mercy is the story of the religious conversion to Christianity of a drunken tavern brawler with the appropriate name of Saul Kane. His conversion, like St. Paul's, is violent, sudden, and unexpected; but Masefield believed that all men, regardless of station or lack of education, were worthy of salvation and had the capacity for forgiving and being forgiven. Moreover, Masefield believed that all men in all stations were fit subjects for poetry.

In the story, Saul Kane narrates an account of the first twenty-six years of his life in the opening three stanzas. The reader learns of his fight on Woodtop Field with a fellow poacher, Billy Myers, his old friend, because both had tried to poach the same territory. In fact, the "right" was with Bill; for the field was his territory. After

Saul wins the boxing match, his backers who have won money on his victory wish to fete him at the pub. He goes with them, but the cool evening air, a rising poetical sense of the history and the meaning of his childhood market town with its old church, a growing realization that he has wronged a friend and fought for a lie, and a quickening recognition of the meaninglessness of his life cause him to recognize his drunken swinishness and the vileness of his companions and surroundings in the pub. Literally, he needs air; and, spiritually, he craves the wind of salvation:

> I opened window wide and leaned
> Out of the pigstye of the fiend
> And felt a cool wind go like grace
> About the sleeping market-place.
> The clock struck three, and sweetly, slowly,
> The bells chimed Holy, Holy, Holy:

Rejecting the devil, Saul becomes a prophet Elijah who begins a rampaging crusade against hypocrisy for one mad, glorious night. After he pulls off his clothes while seeking, like Lear, the truth of his poverty and mortality, he runs screaming through the darkened town with blazing lamps in each hand like the very meteor of the Fall:

> A blaze of flame behind me streamed,
> And then I clashed the lamps and screamed
> "I'm Satan, newly come from hell."
> And then I spied the fire-bell

The fire-bell blasts, the town is in panic, and the firemen and their horses pour into the street and chase the naked madman through the village. Saul outruns them all; and, after returning to the Lion Inn to locate his filthy clothes, he sleeps off his drunkenness. The next night, drunk again, he takes on the Parson, as a representative of the establishment, in fruitless argument. A meeting with a Quaker lady moves him, but nothing really affects him until in the morning the mercy of Christ comes to him in the image of the patient, spiritual plowman:

> Near Bullen Bank, on Gloucester Road
> Thy everlasting mercy showed
> The ploughman patient on the hill

> For ever there, for ever still,
> Ploughing the hill with steady yoke
> Of pine-trees lightning-struck and broke.

Saul Kane, the sinner, a provincial Everyman, has seen Christ as perhaps only the sinner can. His seemingly irrevocable path to damnation has been halted "by the sting of sudden perception of the world around him."[5] Saul's capacity for passion, greater even than his capacity for ale, is the very quality through which God works in man. Passion, a barometer of a man's life force, is for Masefield the power and the glory of human existence. Good and evil war mightily to control the passion of Saul Kane and every other human being. In fact, *The Everlasting Mercy* presents a vivid contrast of light and dark to support the almost Manichaean conflict between good and evil. The effect is not subtle nor is it intended to be. The characters and the environment are stark and not shaded. "Night and sin are black; dawn and the new path which opens before the converted Saul are a blinding white."[6]

The Everlasting Mercy's punch is one of the delights of the poem. It opens in a no-nonsense way.

> From '41 to '51
> I was my folk's contrary son;
> I bit my father's hand right through
> And broke my mother's heart in two.

When the former friends, Saul and Bill, have their falling out, Masefield brilliantly manages to contain their natural expression with all their vigor within the bounds of his verse form, couplets of iambic tetrameter:

> Now when he saw me set my snare,
> He tells me "Get to hell from there.
> This field is mine," he says "by right;
> If you poach her, there'll be a fight.
> Out now," he says, "and leave your wire;
> It's mine."
>   "It ain't."
>   "You put."
>   "You liar."

When Saul later goes berserk, the reader rushes along in the exciting exuberant torrent of his action. The very rhythms of the poem carry the reader with Saul in an empathetic engagement with the tormented protagonist:

> At that I tore my clothes in shreds
> and hurled them on the window leads;
> I flung my boots through both the winders
> And knocked the glass to little flinders;
> The punch bowl and the tumblers followed,
> And then I seized the lamps and holloed,
> And down the stairs, and tore back bolts,
> As mad as twenty blooded colts;
> And out into the street I pass,
> As mad as two-year-olds at grass,
> A naked madman waving grand
> A blazing lamp in either hand.

Another particularly successful aspect of *The Everlasting Mercy* is the localizing of the action to the Ledbury, Herefordshire, area of England in such a way as to make the poem magnificently evocative of late nineteenth-century English country life. The very beauty of the landscape is a factor and a force in the conversion of the pagan Saul to decent Christian life. As Saul approaches the morning of his salvation, he sees his country world as a place of joyous beauty; indeed, it is the Paradise of his deepest dream:

> "It's dawn," I said, "and chimney's smoking,
> And all the blessed fields are soaking.
> It's dawn, and there's an engine shunting;
> And hounds, for huntsman's going hunting.
> It's dawn, and I must wander north
> Along the road Christ led me forth."
>
> So up the road I wander slow
> Past where the snowdrops used to grow
> With celandines in early springs,
> When rainbows were triumphant things
> And dew so bright and flowers so glad,
> Eternal joy to lass and lad.
> And past the lovely brook I paced,
> The brook whose source I never traced,
> The brook, the one of two which rise
> In my green dream in Paradise,
> In wells where heavenly buckets clink

To give God's wandering thirsty drink
By those clean cots of carven stone
Where the clear water sings alone.
Then down, past that white-blossomed pond,
And past the chestnut trees beyond,
And past the bridge the fishers knew,
Where yellow flag flowers once grew,
Where we'd go gathering cops of clover,
In sunny June times long since over.
O clover-cops half white, half red,
O beauty from beyond the dead.
O blossom, key to earth and heaven,
O soul that Christ has new forgiven.

It must be noted that the landscape, the town, and the way of life which Masefield depicts in such works as *The Everlasting Mercy* and *The Widow in the Bye Street* are not to be seen or found in Britain today any more than Thomas Hardy's Wessex and its customs are as Hardy depicted them. Masefield was writing about an England before the automobile, the superhighway, the urban sprawl, and the modern methods of agriculture. Indeed, the England of his narrative poems did not exist even in the days in which he wrote them; instead, his descriptions reflect the memory of his childhood upbringing in peaceful and lovely rural England of the 1880s. This fact must be kept in mind if one is going to be able to accept the subject of *The Everlasting Mercy* as plausible.

The Everlasting Mercy is, after all, something of an old-fashioned morality play—one in which a properly named Quaker lady, Miss Bourne, could sermonize against drink and help save through Christ's intervention a swearing drunkard who was a long way down the road to damnation. Although such a world was perhaps a naive one, such unsophistication that allowed a man to have a vision and to be saved was part of the charm and the goodness of a world for which Masefield and so many of his readers nostalgically longed. That world—before the collective welfare state, before the great totalitarianism of the twentieth century, before mass exterminations of human beings in the name of ideology—could believe that an individual human soul, even that of a man in the lowliest station, was infinitely precious and that God would take the greatest of pains (even to the extent of appearing to the sinner) in order to save that single precious soul from damnation.

Saul Kane believes that the sight of a single farmer was the very image of Christ at work opening up the souls of men for salvation:

> Up the slow slope a team came bowing,
> Old Callow at his autumn ploughing,
> Old Callow, stooped above the hales,
> Ploughing the stubble into wales;
> His grave eyes looking straight ahead,
> Shearing a long straight furrow red;
> His plough-foot high to give it earth
> To bring new food for men to birth.
>
> . . . .
>
> Slow up the hill the plough team plod,
> Old Callow at the task of God,
> Helped by man's wit, helped by the brute
> Turning a stubborn clay to fruit.

A sinner in the England of Masefield's childhood could fall to his knees in full belief before a vision and turn his life away from Satan and toward Christ:

> I kneeled there in the muddy fallow,
> I knew that Christ was there with Callow,
> That Christ was standing there with me,
> That Christ had taught me what to be,
> That I should plough, and as I ploughed
> My Saviour Christ would sing aloud,
> And as I drove the clods apart
> Christ would be ploughing in my heart,
> Through rest-harrow and bitter roots,
> Through all my bad life's rotten fruits.
>
> O Christ who holds the open gate,
> O Christ who drives the furrow straight,
> O Christ, the plough, O Christ, the laughter
> Of holy white birds flying after. . . .

This final vision of Saul Kane is the culmination to what F. Berry calls the "marvelous precision" in which Masefield traces "the psychology of conversion."[7] Masefield understood and was able to portray deftly the tensions, conflicts, exhaustions, and violent reactions that precipitate the *peripeteia* or reversal that spins a man around and makes a Communist of a reactionary, a teetotaler of an alcoholic, a pacifist of a soldier, or even a believer of an atheist.

Masefield chose not to make the conflict in the poem one between reason and passion as perhaps most twentieth-century authors might have. Masefield, like a pre-1900 writer, decided to make the central conflict of *The Everlasting Mercy* the conflict between body and soul; and, in doing so, he aligned himself with the tradition of folk literature and theology. *The Everlasting Mercy* is akin to the English morality play of the fifteenth century and not to the scholastic debates at Oxford and Cambridge in the same period, just as it is related to and a descendant from the chapel and revivalist sermons of the nineteenth century and not of the intellectual tomes of the Church of England of the same period.

Ultimately, *The Everlasting Mercy* is a confession, a poor man's St. Augustine's. Saul Kane is speaking, perhaps sermonizing after the fact; and he is exhorting his fellow countrymen to avoid the pitfalls he fell into and to learn from his experience. He continually interjects into his narrative such personal remarks as "Now, friends, observe and look upon me, / Mark how the Lord took pity on me." Since Saul Kane's faith has always been there, his conversion is not to something new but to that quality and that grace which are within him. For Masefield, a man like Kane is as worth saving as any mighty prince or merchant; and the poem preaches the equality of man before God if not before the state. Finally, *The Everlasting Mercy* is an historical document as well as a religious one, for it chronicles and manifests the high point of nineteenth-century English evangelical revivalism for a twentieth-century reading public that was rapidly losing touch with the power and the meaning of that movement.

II   The Widow in the Bye Street

The Widow in the Bye Street (1912) is a compassionate tale about a poor woman and her only son who was hanged for a crime of passion. The widow, a virtuous but overprotective mother, has reared a fine upstanding son, Jimmy Gurney, to manhood. But also living in the "little Shropshire town" are a beautiful, immoral young widow named Anna, who has borne two children but has smothered one and abandoned the other, and the shepherd Ern, who is a treacherous, philandering wife-beater. Ern and Anna are lovers.

The October fair brings these lives together and subjects them to
the hand of fate.

Anna's ride to the fair is late; and Ern, angry because he thinks
he has been neglected, consorts with the pretty gypsy, Bessie. When
Anna sees her lover and his new girl friend together, she is jealous.
She sees young Jimmy wrestling a ram in a contest; and, posing as a
virtuous maiden, she worms her way into the affections of the innocent young man and, for a while, even into the good graces of the
widow. Mrs. Gurney, however, soon fears that Jimmy will no longer
support her if he takes up with a woman. When Jimmy begins to
court Anna with presents he can ill afford, she takes everything and
gives nothing in return. When his mother sets herself against Anna,
she hardens Jimmy's determination to win Anna. Meanwhile, the
young man's work as a day laborer suffers because he daydreams
and reports in late; and he soon loses his job.

Ern, having made Bessie pregnant, sends her back in misery to
her tribe and returns to his unfortunate wife. Anna, learning of his
return, wants him back. She parades, with the unsuspecting Jimmy,
repeatedly past Ern's house; and, when the shepherd finally con-
fronts the couple, Anna indicates her preference for Ern, to Jimmy's
anger. After Ern and Anna have again become lovers, Jimmy gets
drunk; goes to Anna's house; and, in a fit of passionate anger, kills
Ern with a "plough-bat" found in a field. Although Jimmy never
meant to kill his rival, he nevertheless is convicted and hanged.
Anna goes off with another romantic tale in her repertoire, and the
widow is left in madness and poverty.

The Widow in the Bye Street, like *The Everlasting Mercy.* relies
to a great extent upon the English countryside for background,
mood, and power. The cottage of the poor widow and her laborer
son is finely drawn; the dialect is carefully and accurately tuned;
and Masefield presents two particularly colorful and convincing
scenes: the October fair and the Assize session. The countryside is
particularly peaceful in this poem, for nature in Masefield's world
of the narrative does not in its elements reflect the storms within the
hearts and souls of men and women as it does so often in
Shakespeare. Rather, the countryside is the continuum and the
norm; and in its placidity it contrasts with man's passions. The
scenery comes to life in spring even as Jimmy hangs, a useless fruit
on the hangman's tree.

Nature is greater than man, who is such a small part of the plan.
When Jimmy has been rejected by Anna and tramps off into the

countryside consumed with disgust and anger, he comes to a small stream:

> . . . . He sat him down to rage,
> Beside the stream whose waters never age.
>
> Plashing, it slithered down the tiny fall
> To eddy wrinkles in the trembling pool
> With that light voice whose music cannot pall,
> Always the note of solace, flute-like, cool.
> And when hot-headed man has been a fool,
> He could not do a wiser thing than go
> To that dim pool where purple teazles grow.

The moral of the sermon in the running brook is clear for the reader if, tragically, it is unclear to Jimmy: the fire in the soul can be cooled in contemplation and in communion with the beauty and permanence of the creation. When the corrupt but still beautiful Anna returns home from the trial, the train descends, other life goes on, oblivious to Jimmy's imminent suffering and death. Again Nature shows her indifference to human tragedy.

> Into the vale and halts and starts to climb
> To where the apple-bearing country ends
> And pleasant-pastured hills rise sweet with thyme,
> When clinking sheepbells make a broken chime
> And sunwarm gorses rich the air with scent
> And kestrels poise for mice, there Anna went.
>
> There, in the April, in the garden-close,
> One heard her in the morning singing sweet,
> Calling the birds from the unbudded rose,
> Offering her lips with grains for them to eat.
> The redbreasts come with little wiry feet,
> Sparrows and tits and all wild feathery things,
> Brushing her lifted face with quivering wings.

Even after the execution, when the widow wanders like a mad Ophelia over the countryside, she is singing the song she once sang with her son; but she too finds peace in nature:

> The stars are placid on the evening's blue,
> Burning like eyes so calm, so unafraid,
> On all that God has given and man has made.

Burning they watch, and mothlike owls come out,
The redbreast warbles shrilly once and stops;
The homing cowman gives his dog a shout,
The lamps are lighted in the village shops.
Silence; the last bird passes; in the copse
The hazels cross the moon, a nightjar spins,
Dew wets the grass, the nightingale begins.

Singing her crazy song the mother goes,
Singing as though her heart were full of peace,
Moths knock the petals from the dropping rose,
Stars make the glimmering pool a golden fleece,
The moon droops west, but still she does not cease,
The little mice peep out to hear her sing,
Until the inn-man's cockerel shakes his wing.

Professor F. Berry has noted the very particular relationship between *The Widow in the Bye Street* and Chaucer's "Prioress's Tale."[8] Most obviously, Masefield uses Chaucer's seven-line, rhyme-royal stanza; but beyond this similarity, and much more significantly, Masefield's skill in achieving pathos in the poem is Chaucerian and his casting of events to spin the web of his tale approaches the skill of England's ancient storyteller. The "Prioress's Tale" opens with the setting of place within a community and so does *The Widow in the Bye Street*. Chaucer's poem was about a widow's son who was murdered as is Masefield's, albeit it is society who murders him. The beautiful relationship between mother and son is set out early in both poems, and the similarities continue.

Like *The Everlasting Mercy*, *The Widow in the Bye Street* is a poem with strong moral overtones. The sermon of this work is not the message that all men, even the lowliest, may be saved. Here Masefield strongly attacks capital punishment in a system of justice which can deprive a good young man of his useful life for a moment's act of unpremeditated passion. But pathos turns to tragedy in the realization of man's inhumanity to man committed in the name of justice. A bell rings out an indifferent warning, quite inadequate to the enormity of the crime against life, when Jimmy is about to be executed:

The broken ringing clanged, clattered and clanged
As though men's bees were swarming, not men hanged.

Now certain Justice with the pitiless knife.
The white sick chaplain snuffling at the nose,

"I am the resurrection and the life. '
The bell still clangs, the small procession goes,
The prison warders ready ranged in rows.
"Now, Gurney, come, my dear; it's time," they said.
And ninety seconds later he was dead.

Masefield's revulsion over capital punishment is quite clear. Surely *The Widow in the Bye Street*, considering its wide popularity, was another brick in the slowly rising edifice of the collective British conscience which would lead to the abolition of capital punishment.

Though not as striking nor as shocking as *The Everlasting Mercy*, *The Widow in the Bye Street* is a very fine narrative that offers much of the effect of a good novel. It communicates directly and superbly. Although apparently not based on an actual event, it is still indebted to the great tradition of the English journalistic ballad which, from the sixteenth to the eighteenth century, was a means for the dissemination of contemporary domestic news and a folk expression of the collective conscience of a maturing people. If Masefield's narratives are some of Britain's last manifestation of the Chaucerian verse tale, *The Widow in the Bye Street* is probably one of the last serious poems in English that is clearly in the tradition of the anonymous news ballad.

The Everlasting Mercy and *The Widow in the Bye Street* are both tales of violence: a brawl, a rampage, murder in passion, and execution. It is as if these pre-World War I poems, surprisingly flowing from the pen of a peaceful lover of beauty, were artistic foreshadowings of the unprecedented world violence that was so soon to explode. The popularity of Masefield's and Kipling's poems and of Jack London's novels just before the war may have been due to their unconscious sensing of the lemming-like cascade to mass violence that was just beginning.

III Dauber

In *Dauber* (1913), Masefield returns to his other "landscape," the sea. This tale, "a parable of trial,"[9] is a vision of life and art as a struggle to survive in dignity and with worthiness in the storms of ignorance, prejudice, and hatred. *Dauber* is as successful a narrative poem as *The Everlasting Mercy* in respect to characterization and suspense. It expresses "in a fable the conflict which was troubling Masefield; a peculiarly English conflict which he was to resolve later. It is the story of a man sensitive to beauty, set in a community which is hostile or at least indifferent to everything that he

values."[10] Dauber, a young man whose real name is Joe, goes to sea
because he wishes to capture on canvas the beauty of ships under
sail and the power of deep water. He plans to spend three years
before the mast as an apprentice seaman and as an apprentice
painter. Because all of his free time is spent drawing and painting,
the mate takes a dislike to Joe and contemptuously nicknames him
"Dauber."

After Dauber has hidden his work beneath a longboat on the
deckhouse top, two of the crew find it and ruin it with turpentine.
Dauber, furious, finds his tormentors who admit their deeds and
urge Dauber to complain to the captain; but the captain merely
reprimands him for stowing his paintings under the boat. During a
rain squall, Dauber begins a friendship with Si, one of the young
men who had ruined his paintings, and tells him of his poor rural
origins, how he had felt the farm to be a prison, how he had discovered his mother's drawings and had also started to paint. When
the mate learns that Si, who is in training to be an officer, has been
conversing with Dauber, an ordinary seaman, he orders Dauber's
new friend never to speak to the artist again. If Si does so, he will be
dismissed from officer's training and forced to bunk forward with
the men.

As a result of the mate's enmity, Dauber is isolated once more.
The men continue to taunt him and ruin his work, but he nonetheless persists in his painting. When the ship approaches the ever
treacherous Cape Horn, Dauber dreads the fact that he must soon
go aloft to help with the sails despite his inexperience. Yet he deter-
mines to prove himself a seaman at the Horn—to indicate that he
can contribute to the communal needs of the society of a ship
struggling for survival. While the vessel survives thirty days of the
cruelest weather, Dauber achieves manhood in the eyes of the crew
and in his own eyes during the passage. When the ship is seemingly
clear of foul weather and on its way to Valparaiso, it is hit once
more by a storm. When Dauber goes aloft, he falls to his death; and
his last words are "It will go on." When his body is committed to
the sea, the sea god acts as if he had been waiting for an offering
from the vessel, for the weather turns fair and the ship makes port.

Dauber is a tragedy in which an artist, who chose to prove
himself in a sphere of activity for which he had no ability and in
which the world expected him to make that effort, loses his life and
the world loses his talent. Although Dauber's death is justifiable in
his own eyes and perhaps even in those of the seamen, Dauber has

proved his manhood and his right to equal treatment in a hard
world; nevertheless, his death has no ultimate meaning for society.
Another man could have handled the sails much more easily, and
another man might have been more easily spared by the world.
Since artists are few enough as it is, Dauber's is the same old
senseless death of the gifted in the trenches or fox-holes of brutal,
machine-run wars that are best fought by professionals.

Masefield begins *Dauber* in fine Chaucerian fashion with the
scene set and the painter introduced:

> Four bells were struck, the watch was called on deck,
> All work aboard was over for the hour,
> And some men sang and others played at check,
> Or mended clothes or watched the sunset glower.
> The bursting west was like an opening flower,
> And one man watched it till the light was dim,
> But no one went across to talk to him.
>
> He was the painter in that swift ship's crew—
> Lampman and painter—tall, a slight-built man,
> Young for his years, and not yet twenty-two;
> Sickly, and not yet brown with the sea's tan.
> Bullied and damned at since the voyage began,
> "Being neither man nor seaman by his tally,"
> He bunked with the idlers just abaft the galley.

This tough beginning is, like the rest of the poem, without sentimentality. It is only in Dauber's romantic fallacy—his belief that
an artist must participate in experience in order to record it or understand it—that the iron plating of the poem rusts through to
reveal a spot of softness:

> Si talked with Dauber, standing by the side,
> "Why did you come to sea, painter?" he replied,
> "I want to be a painter," he replied,
> "And know the sea and ships from A to Z,
> And paint great ships at sea before I'm dead;
> Ships under skysails running down the Trade—
> Ships and the sea; there's nothing finer made.
>
> "But there's so much to learn, with sails and ropes,
> And how the sails look, full or being furled,
> And how the lights change in the troughs and slopes,
> And the sea's colours up and down the world,

> And how a storm looks when the sprays are hurled
> High as the yard (they say) I want to see;
> There's none ashore can teach such things to me.

The painter's sensitivity, so alien to his shipmates, is stroked home with concise, powerful, imagistic language:

> Even as he spoke his busy pencil moved,
> Drawing the leap of water off the side
> Where the great clipper trampled iron-hooved,
> Making the blue hills of the sea divide,
> Shearing a glittering scatter in her stride,
> And leaping on full tilt with all sails drawing,
> Proud as a war-horse, snuffling battle, pawing.

> "I cannot get it yet—not yet," he said;
> "That leap and light, and sudden change to green,
> And all the glittering from the sunset's red,
> And the milky colours where the bursts have been,
> And then the clipper striding like a queen
> Over it all, all beauty to the crown.
> I see it all, I cannot put it down.

The ship and the sailors try to destroy or dismiss this alien being from their midst because the artist is superfluous to their needs and a threat to their values. The vessel herself seems at first to be Dauber's antagonist and then slowly accepts the intertwining of his destiny with hers. She seems to be the first to realize that the artist-Jonah must be sacrificed for her survival and that of the ship-society. When Dauber is given the foghorn watch on the bow as the fog closes in and the storm portends, he sounds the notes of doom:

> Denser it grew, until the ship was lost.
> The elemental hid her; she was merged
> In mufflings of dark death, like a man's ghost,
> New to the change of death, yet thither urged.
> Then from the hidden waters something surged—
> Mournful, despairing, great, greater than speech,
> A noise like one slow wave on a still beach.

Only the whales, lonely mammals in a hostile sea and outcasts of the earth like Dauber, answer through the mist.

Masefield is at his descriptive best when the gale hits the vessel, sails rip, yards and tackle tumble, and Dauber goes aloft in terror to

furl sail and, by so doing, proves his courage and attests his
manhood in the eyes of the bosun. In this passage which is as
evocative, as brilliant, and as exciting as Conrad's prose account of
the great storm in *Typhoon*, Dauber the sailor conflicts with Dauber
the artist. Masefield seems to feel that a man cannot be a man of action and a man of art at the same time, for the artist died in the first
storm as the man was born. The seaman will die in the second storm
for the ship must have her blood sacrifice before she will allow, or
the sea will allow her, safe anchor. When Dauber falls to his death,
he hardly realizes what is happening. He thinks another man is falling, not he. When the men gather around his body they mourn him
not as an artist but as the "smart young seaman he was getting to
be." The world mourns its doers not its dreamers, but art will "go
on."

With Dauber's Jonah-like sacrifice, the winds fall and turn fair.
In one of Masefield's most lovely passages, the men reach safety as
the land reaches out to them like the long hand of salvation:

> Then in the sunset's flush they went aloft
> And unbent sails in that most lovely hour
> When the light gentles and the wind is soft
> And beauty in the heart breaks like a flower.
> Working aloft they saw the mountain tower,
> Snow to the peak; they heard the launchmen shout;
> And bright along the bay the lights came out.

Dauber is one of the finest narrative poems in the English
language. The seaman-painter, so much like Masefield, himself the
seaman-poet, is a superbly drawn and realized character. The
character and the poem ring with authenticity, but the breath of
creation is in them. Masefield, like all seamen, loves the language of
the seafarers that sets them aside, proclaims their difference, states
their manly craft-wise values, and is their holy tongue as they serve
the gods of the sea. This ancient, traditional, and intrinsically poetic
Masefield uses even more successfully in *Dauber* than in his early
poems, making great and timeless poetry. *Dauber* is "a poem of
genius, one of the great storm-pieces of modern literature. . . ."[11]

IV The Daffodil Fields

Masefield was, however, writing too much, for *The Daffodil*

Fields (1913) was published in the same year as *Dauber*. With a plot as complicated as any novel and with the characterization and the resolution typical of melodramas, *The Daffodil Fields* had a less than enthusiastic reception from critics and is today considered one of Masefield's weaker major narratives. The poem is the tale of three friends—Michael Gray, Mary Keir, and Lion Occleve—who become involved in a fatal love triangle. As the story begins, the friends are in their youth; and Michael's father, who is dying, calls his friends, the fathers of Mary and Lion, and gets them to agree to guide and help his wild son, whom he is leaving penniless. Michael returns from school in Paris, from which he has just been expelled for misbehavior, in time to mourn over his father's body. Mary loves him, but Lion loves Mary.

Michael decides to go abroad to seek his fortune by the River Platte in South America. Before leaving, he becomes infatuated with Mary, they become engaged, and Michael promises to return within three years. He leaves, finds little success, never writes to Mary, and is soon consoled near the River Platte with another love. Mary remains faithful to him despite the fact that he never writes to her. When her father is killed in a riding accident, the ever-faithful Lion helps her to settle her affairs; but she still waits.

Meanwhile, when Lion's prize bull-calf is bought by an Argentine rancher, he travels to the River Platte to deliver the animal and to seek Michael on behalf of the woman he himself loves since Michael's three promised years have passed. Although Lion finds Michael living with his new love, a dark Spanish beauty, he asks him to return to sorrowing Mary in Shropshire. After Michael refuses to do so, Lion returns to England, finally persuades Mary of the futility of her wait for Michael, and they marry. After Mary has sent her wedding announcement to Michael, he perversely starts aching for her when he realizes she is lost to him. He works his way home to England, where Mary and Lion seem to have found peace. As soon as Michael is back, however, Mary realizes that she still loves him passionately; and she abandons Lion to live with Michael.

Distracted by the loss of his wife, Lion seeks to confront Michael with his sin. Michael has a message for Lion, who now furious, refuses to listen; and they fight to the death in the field of daffodils. As they are dying, their brotherhood reasserts itself; and Michael tells his friend that he was on the way to inform him that Mary and he had decided that she should return to Lion. Lion dies with the realization that he has needlessly caused the death of his friend as well as his own. Mary comes upon the scene in time to bid farewell; the bodies are laid out together at the Occleves; and Mary, after gathering daffodils for the deathbed, dies of a broken heart with her head falling on Michael's breast. The scene shifts to the outer world where sailors recall "this old tale of woe among the daffodils."

In *The Daffodil Fields*, a potboiler, Masefield made such a poor choice of situation for his narrative that his skill at versification, his successful evocation of the Shropshire countryside and a South American landscape, as well as his storytelling ability, could not save the poem. He failed when trying to make a rather common love triangle into a Hardyesque tragedy in verse, primarily because the implausibility of the ever-suffering and ever-waiting Mary and Lion creates melodrama.

The best aspect of *The Daffodil Fields* is Masefield's use of the iterative daffodil image as a means of structuring the story and of adding thematic significance to a prosaic tale of unrequited love and adultery. The poem contains some thirty references to daffodils which represent eternal nature and which appear at the beginning of the poem along with a description of the lovely farms of Shropshire. These flowers are lovely in the moonlight when Lion and Mary meet Michael after his return from France. When Michael leaves for South America, Mary sobs in the withered field of daffodils; and their blooming and waning mark the passing years of Michael's absence. Because the very land of the Argentine is distinguished in its difference and in its distance from England as being "Far from the daffodil field . . . ," the symbol takes on the value of the eternal English countryside in a true Wordsworthian aspect. Finally, the daffodils are spattered with the blood of the young men, and Mary covers their bodies with daffodils and other flowers. The last word of the poem, incongruously preceded by a barrage of seafaring images in the final stanza, is "daffodils."

This poem marks the beginning of Masefield's serious interest in Latin America and especially with the juxtaposition presented by Englishmen living and working in that seemingly more exotic part of the world. This interest, which blossomed in Masefield's novels of the 1920s and 1930s, perhaps came about in part because of Conrad's artistic success with *Nostromo* (1904), for Masefield had no personal experience with South America beyond his early sailing days.

V Reynard the Fox

Six years and the most terrible war that the world had known came between *The Daffodil Fields* and Masefield's next narrative *Reynard the Fox* (1919). During the war years, the English-speaking literary world had admired Masefield's personal and literary contributions to the war effort. His poem "August 1914," to be discussed later, was so much admired that it was considered by some critics to be the best "war" poem of the 1914-1918 encounter. Masefield's war histories, which at the least were masterpieces of journalism, were standard reading fare for Englishmen. After World War I had ended, the reading public expected a poetic or a fictional synthesis of the trials of war. Masefield, who chose not to produce such a work disappointed his public and his critics. Instead, he wrote his finest narrative poem, *Reynard the Fox*.

Amy Lowell, who understood that Masefield was reacting to the war in his own way, rightly regarded *Reynard the Fox* as "a cry of hunger for the past, a wave of nostalgic longing for the old, simple, thoughtless days of security and peace."[12] In fact, the subject, the setting, the Chaucerian possibilities, the inherent struggle between hunter and hunted, the cinematic chase, the underdog's (fox's) escape, and the poets' highly tuned power as a narrative poet all served to bring Masefield to a point of inspiration and creativity he never again reached.

To many critics, *Reynard the Fox* captures the quintessence of Englishness: "the music of English names, and above all, an Englishness, a feeling for the English scene which has no parallel outside the grandest of English country poems: all these qualities combine smoothly to make a poem which is the peak of Masefield's achievement and puts him among the great. We must look back to Chaucer for a like simplicity and effortless evocation of our countryside: and, in this poem, Masefield stands near his master."[13]

J. Middleton Murry concluded begrudgingly that Masefield had "reached a point at which his mannerisms have been so subdued that they no longer sensibly impeded the movement of his verse, a point at which we may begin to speak (though not too loud) of mastery."[14] Murry is quite wrong, however, when he calls *Reynard the Fox* "an epic of fox-hunting" for the narrative is not an apology for the blood sport nor is it a polemic against the cruelty of hunting. Masefield makes no moral judgment in that respect, for the hunt is merely the means by which he is able to create the most exquisitely detailed and precise moving panorama of the English countryside at the turn of the century. The hunt is the central architectonic action of a vast, moving painting in the same way that the pilgrimage is the central architectonic action in the *Canterbury Tales.*

A good way for the serious reader to approach *Reynard the Fox* is through Masefield's essay "Fox-Hunting" in *Recent Prose.* First, this essay tells the reader why Masefield chose the subject:

> At a fox-hunt, and nowhere else in England, except perhaps at a funeral, can you see the whole of the land's society brought together, focussed [*sic*] for the observer, as the Canterbury pilgrims were for Chaucer.
> This fact made the subject attractive. The fox-hunt gave an opportunity for a picture or pictures of the members of an English community.[15]

Second, the hunt was a part of Masefield's childhood experience. He was not a participator but rather a spectator of the pageant and ritual of the sport: "Often as a little child, I saw and heard hounds hunting in and near a covert within sight of my old home. Once, when I was, perhaps, five years old, the fox was hunted into our garden, and those glorious beings in scarlet, as well as the hounds, were all about my lairs, like visitants from Paradise. The fox, on this occasion, went through a wood-shed, and escaped."[16]

Like Reynard, the fox of Masefield's childhood cleverly escapes the whole flying institution. Also significant is the poet's reference to "Paradise," for this key word in Masefield's work begins to emerge as meaning the rural English countryside of Masefield's nostalgia. To the end of his creative life "Paradise" and the late nineteenth-century rural England are so frequently compared that they finally merge into one metaphor and one symbol.

Third, the essay indicates Masefield's quite typical Anglo-Saxon sympathy for the underdog, for *Reynard the Fox* is not a poem about victory but about survival. The fox must persevere against overwhelming odds—against an army of snapping, bone-crushing jaws. Victory has no meaning for him: he cannot destroy his enemies; he must survive by cunning. Masefield seems to imply that his Reynard is, in the tradition of Aesop, an allegorical figure who represents modern man:

> No fox was the original of my Reynard, but as I was much in the woods as a boy, I saw foxes fairly often, considering that they are night-moving animals. Their grace, beauty, cleverness and secrecy always thrilled me.

Then that kind of grin which the mask wears made me credit them with an almost human humour. I thought the fox a merry devil, though a bloody one. Then he is one against many, who keeps his end up, and lives, often snugly, in spite of the world. The pirate and the night rider are nothing to the fox, for romance and danger.[17]

When Masefield penned a brief introduction to the 1962 edition of the poem, he finally verbalized the allegorical value of the pursued fox as the spirit of European man which, by a hair's breadth, had survived World War I when sorely pursued by Death for four long years through most of the Continent. "It had survived the chase, but as a hunted fox may survive a long run, to lie panting somewhere till the heart stops beating. It was my hope that my Fox's heart should not stop beating."[18]

Reynard the Fox; or *The Ghost Heath Run* is a poem in two parts. Part I is the human tale in which a hunting meet takes place at "The Cock and Pye," a three hundred-year-old inn owned by Charles and Martha Enderby. The first part of the poem describes the people who come to the meet and briefly tells a part of the story of each. This section could be called the "Prelude to Reynard the Fox", for each vignette is in a Chaucerian picture like those in the Prelude to the *Canterbury Tales* except that Masefield deals with a greater number of people and in less depth. The hunt assembles; the hounds are ready; and, at the word of Sir Peter Bynd of Coombe, the party sets out for Ghost Heath Wood—where Old Baldy Hill says the foxes are lying. Some of the riders think they are going to the wrong place, but Robin Dawe, the huntsman, knows hounds and sees that they are onto a scent saying " 'We'll find . . . a score.' " The hound, Daffodil, gets a fox scent, is after it with wild high crying, and the hounds and men charge into the cover.

Part II tells the tale of a three-year-old fox—bred "On old cold Crendon's windy tops" who scents a vixen in heat, follows the scent to Ghost Heath Wood, not aware that men who "were devils" were on the hunt and that "The world [was in a state of] one lust for a fox's blood." The hunters get a line on his scent, the fox flees, the men pursue, and people on the fox's escape-path note his passage.

The fox tries to lose his pursuers by running through manure to kill his scent and by then outrunning them to a safe haven. The first maneuver doesn't work; and, when he reaches his lair on Wan Dyke Hill, he finds his hole stopped up and barred with stakes. He remembers another hole—a rabbit hole—but a rabbit hunter is there. The rabbit hunter's terrier puppy takes up the fox-chase; and the fox, now tired, dragging and desperate, finds that the terrier's chase has killed his scent. The fox regains some of his strength, but the hounds find him again by scent and the pursuit is resumed. They run over open country, and the race has marathon proportions. At last the fox reaches the Mourne End Wood, leaps a thorn barrier, spurts through the woods to the Mourne End rocks, and finally goes to earth in a rabbit meuse, where he had played as a fox kit with his "mates."

The hounds and hunters never come for him; and, when the stars are bright, he returns home to "Old Cold Crendon and Hilcote Copse." Meanwhile, the hunters and hounds return to the "Cock" at dusk, having caught another fox. They had picked up a different scent in Mourne End Wood and had run the second fox to earth and killed it. They talk about the hunt and are not sure if the fox they caught was the one they had started hunting, but they do know that the day's hunt is one they will never forget.

Masefield's imagination creates a magnificent group of character vignettes in Part I, like that of Old Steven:

> . . . from Scratch Steven place
> (A white beard and a rosy face)
> Came next on his stringhalty grey.
> 'I've come to see the hounds away,'
> He said, 'and ride a field or two.
> We old have better things to do
> Than breaking all our necks for fun.'
> He shone on people like the sun,
> And on himself for shining so.

and, like Chaucer, Masefield also has a parson:

> The parson was a manly one,
> His jolly eyes were bright with fun.
> His jolly mouth was well inclined
> To cry aloud his jolly mind
> To everyone, in jolly terms.
> He did not talk of churchyard worms,
> But of our privilege as dust
> To box a lively bout with lust
> Ere going to heaven to rejoice.
> He loved the sound of his own voice,

His talk was like a charge of horse;
His build was all compact, for force,
Well-knit, well-made, well-coloured, eager.
He kept no Lent to make him meagre,
He loved his God, himself and man.
He never said, "life's wretched span;
This wicked world." in any sermon.
This body that we feed the worm on,
To him, was jovial stuff that thrilled.
He liked to see the foxes killed;
But most he felt himself in clover
To hear, 'Hen left, hare right, cock over.'
At woodside, when the leaves are brown.
Some grey cathedral in a town
Where drowsy bells toll out the time
To shaven closes sweet with lime,
And wall-flower roots drive out of the mortar
All summer on the Norman Dortar
Was certain some day to be his.
Nor would a mitre go amiss
To him, because he governed well.
His voice was like the tenor bell
When services were said and sung,
And he had read in many a tongue,
Arabic, Hebrew, Spanish, Greek.

One after another, the men and women of a long-changed, almost forgotten landscape parade by; and they are more real than historical figures and destined like Chaucer's pilgrims, like Shakespeare's rustics in the history plays, or like Hardy's gloomy farmfolk to mark a time and a place and say "this is how men were."

More story poems came from his pen, but Masefield had reached his "supreme achievement in narrative."[19] *Reynard the Fox* achieved everything Masefield intended to do. He "filmed" with words a superb pageant and a great symbolic chase, and all takes place in one ideal day of brilliant color and excitement. The poem begins at dawn and ends at nightfall: a day selected to stand for all the best days of England's past.

VI   Enslaved

In the next year, 1920, Masefield published two more long narratives, *Enslaved* and *Right Royal*, as well as a great deal of shorter verse. In *Enslaved,* an adventure into the exotic for Masefield, he leaves his familiar environs, the English rural countryside and the sea, and takes the reader to a Moorish caliphate that is probably of the late seventeenth century. Although the time of events is never made clear in the poem, English seapower was temporarily weak and Barbary pirates did raid the coast in the late seventeenth century.

Enslaved is not only Masefield's most exotic major narrative, it is his most erotic. A beautiful English girl is abducted from her seaside home by Moorish slavers who plan to take her to the harem of a Khalif. Her lover, unable to live without her, follows immediately in a small craft, overtakes the pirate vessel, and offers himself to slavery "To be comrade to the woman whom you've dragged away from home./ Since I cannot set her free, I want only to be near her." As one may readily observe, the situation is highly sentimental, and the verse is often barely measured prose. However, the story line is engrossing even though the plot is implausible and the verse is weaker than one expects.

The hero's ordeal in slavery is a terrible one. With a fellow slave, he attempts to rescue his fair damsel; and they kill a traitor in the process. The harem is reached and broached at night; the girl is rescued; but, as the three escapees make for the waterfront, they are discovered, pursued, and captured. A horrible fate looms before them because the Khalif is furious. The hero, magnificent in the face of disaster and defeat as only a Masefield hero can be, says:

> "We did the generous thing and are defeated.
> Boast, then, to-night, when you have drunken deep,
> Between the singing woman's song and sleep,
> That you have tortured to the death three slaves
> Who spat upon your law and found their graves
> Helping each other in the generous thing.
> No mighty triumph for a boast, O King."

Humanity stirs in the hawk's breast of the Khalif; he relents; and the captives, along with another Christian girl for whom the heroine has pleaded, are set free and given a swift vessel to take them home. They, Masefield, and the reader rejoice:

> O beautiful is love and to be free
> Is beautiful, and beautiful are friends.

Love, freedom, comrades, surely make amends
For all these thorns through which we walk to death.
God let us breathe your beauty with our breath.

This paean to beauty, which identifies that attribute or quality with God, is one of Masefield's most succinct statements about what was for him the major source of creativity in the universe and the only quest worth the effort:

> To him Beauty is clearly something very different from the metaphysics of Plato, or the ethics of Ruskin, or the hedonism of Pater, or the dilettante aesthetics of Wilde. To him Beauty must be the one divine thing in this world that we can be sure of, that satisfies, that gives to the soul peace and rest; the one rational restorer of human pride and dignity . . . and finally a great ideal principle able to help its votaries to face and conquer fate and life and the world. This vital principle he finds in many places and relations; it enables him to forget life's intolerable evils, to defy old age, to die content; it is the subject and purpose of all his writing.[20]

Indeed, beauty became Masefield's obsession; it called him eternally although it was really ephemeral and abstract. The heroine of *Enslaved,* despite her beauty, is like so many Masefield lovelies—she never comes to life. But the concept of beauty is in the clouds, in the moving ships on the sea, and in the faces of some women. Beauty, all that is worthwhile for Masefield, is life and the creative spirit. Nonetheless, *Enslaved* was written so hastily that offenses against scansion and euphony exist; flesh and blood seem scarce despite the professed passion; but the story is a good one. The reader, even the modern reader, may have derisive smiles; but he finds himself reading the tale to its bittersweet end and remembering it.

VII   Right Royal

Masefield's *Right Royal* (1920) is stronger than *Enslaved* partly because Masefield is again on home ground. *Right Royal* is not so well crafted nor does it have the scope of *Reynard the Fox*, but this narrative poem is every bit as exciting because it is another chase, another romp, another dash, another cinematic whirl of action. *Right Royal*, a steeplechase horse, is an unreliable animal that was badly trained by his first owner, but the horse possesses great potential for racing success. He has been bought by Charles Cothill, a horseman who believes so much in Right Royal that he mortgages all his earthly possessions to back the horse whom he will ride in the great race, the English Chasers Cup. This rash act precipitates a crisis in Charles' relationship with his betrothed, the golden Emily, whose father had been ruined by racing. Since Emily cannot bear the thought that this ruin could happen to yet another person she loves, their forthcoming marriage and their future happiness are entirely at stake in the race.

Right Royal is by no means the favorite; for, despite his great speed, he has lost several races because of panic and fear, especially of the crowds. He somehow senses, however, the importance of this race to his kind master; and, despite the fact that he falls once and is thirty lengths behind the leader at one point, Right Royal recovers to take Charles on to victory and happiness, even though the man he has bet with defaults on the wager.

Right Royal is the best narrative of a horse race ever written: the poem gallops. The reader is swept along in the excitement and tension. He feels mounted, mud-splattered, and in swift motion.

> Now the race reached the water and over it flew
> In a sweep of great muscle strained taut and guyed true.
> There Muscatel floundered and came to a halt,
> Muscatel, the bay chaser without any fault.
>
> Right Royal's head lifted, Right Royal took charge,
> On the left near the railings, ears cocked, going large,
> Leaving Hadrian behind as a yacht leaves a barge.

Masefield's skill in evoking the atmosphere and action of a steeplechase is remarkable. He has immersed himself in the language, paraphernalia, and procedures of the stable and of racing. The initial description of Right Royal, for example, has the ring of authenticity:

> In a race-course box behind the Stand
> Right Royal shone from a strapper's hand.
> A big dark bay with a restless tread,
> Fetlock deep in a wheat-straw bed;
> A noble horse of a nervy blood,
> By O Mon Roi out of Rectitude.
> Something quick in his eye and ear
> Gave a hint that he might be queer.
> In front, he was all to a horseman's mind;
> Some thought him a trifle light behind.

> By two good points might his rank be known,
> A beautiful head and Jumping Bone.

The poem is by no means profound, for Masefield is not allegoriz-ing as in *Reynard the Fox;* he is content to offer the reader pleasure and excitement. Nonetheless, the best of life was beauty, and man lived better and happier in the company of his fellow humans than alone. Like the sailor he had been and in some ways always re-mained, Masefield most valued the engaged life, serving one's own people in one's own land. The vast mob at a horse race, enjoying itself, caught up in the moment, oblivious to individual mortality, best concretized these values; and Masefield stops in this poem of action for a deeper thought:

> Man who lives under sentence sealed,
> Tragical man, who has but breath
> For few brief years as he goes to death,
> Tragical man by strange winds blown
> To live in crowds ere he die alone,
> Came in his jovial thousands massing
> To see Life moving and beauty passing.

VIII   King Cole

Masefield's last major but not too successful narrative poem was *King Cole* (1921). After this poem, Masefield turned to the novel as the primary medium for his storytelling; and, although he wrote other narrative poems, they lacked the scope and the power of those of 1911-1921 when he reached his high-water mark of poetic ability at the same time that his storytelling skill matured.

King Cole is the story of that mythological good old king who lived so exemplary a life that he was granted as a reward the oppor-tunity to choose his own form of Paradise. Characteristically, he chooses to return to his kingdom and to do good for his fellow man. Since he has great magical power to pursue this end, he

> . . . . wanders shore and shire
> An old, poor, wandering man, with glittering eyes,
> Helping distressful folk to their desire
> By power of spirit that within him lies.
> Gentle he is, and quiet, and most wise,
> He wears a ragged grey, he sings sweet words,
> And where he walks there flutter little birds.

The place is England; the time is not certain but is that of Camelot, King Lear, or simply yesterday. Masefield's story is not complicated, for the fairy tale and children's tale aspect of the legends of King Cole pervade the work. A poor, wet, mud-covered travelling circus arrives in an English town for a planned performance. The circus men are truly down on their luck, for they learn upon arrival that royalty, the Queen and her husband the Prince (Victoria and Albert?), are in the town to lay a foundation stone. The circus must tent in a field a mile from the town where it is unlikely that anyone would come to see them. When King Cole joins the troupe of artists as they approach the community, the ghostly monarch consoles the head showman and his wife who have been in despair and who also miss their estranged, long-lost son.

By magic, King Cole gains audience with the Prince and convinces him to attend the circus with the Queen and the Court. The entire population marches out to the surprised circus. King Cole stands in the ring; and, with the magic of his flute, he transforms the threadbare outfit into a glorious sight, to the delight of all. The circus is a great success; the players are rewarded with a bag of gold; the delighted Queen orders a banquet for the show folk in a nearby tent; and the prodigal son appears. He has been in the army and has served as a sergeant in one of the Queen's regiments. The family is reconciled, and King Cole fades away leaving love and goodwill in his wake.

King Cole evidences some weakening of Masefield's narrative power. The story is strained, the verse is sometimes hobbled, and the characters are neither as abundant nor as well defined as those of the earlier verse narratives. Still there is great charm in the poem, and the circus atmosphere is satisfactorily evocative of that life. One might conjecture that King Cole is Masefield himself—that the poet unconsciously thrust himself and his values into the character of the old monarch; for King Cole is a pleasant piper whose music leads men, creates fantasy and joy. The King has chosen to return from the dead to his choice of Paradise, the English countryside, that was also Masefield's Paradise. King Cole loves and respects artists, especially performing artists, just as Masefield did:

> Yet all of that small troupe in misery stuck,
> Were there by virtue of their nature's choosing
> To be themselves and take the season's luck,
> Counting the being artists worth the bruising.
> To be themselves, as artists, even if losing

> Wealth, comfort, health, in doing as they chose,
> Alone of all life's ways brought peace to those.

Lastly, King Cole's dedication to the service of man and to the doing of good is entirely in keeping with Masefield's bardic concept of the role of the poet.

Masefield's long narratives published between 1911 and 1921 remain his most important work and a major contribution to the history of English poetry. A paragraph he wrote about his master, Chaucer, needs only the substitution of his own name for the ancient's to sum up Masefield's achievement: "Apart from the beauty and the power of the concept, Chaucer is a master story-teller . . . that is, he can hold an audience by the interest of his fable, surprise them by the depth and purity of his sincerity, which speaks from the very heart of his imagined character, win them by living description, and fill their World of Imagination with persons of force and fury, and others of beauty and gentleness."[21]

CHAPTER 4

"*August 1914*" *and Other Poetry*

J OHN Masefield won his fame and his poet laureateship on the strength of his great narrative poems and, to a lesser extent, the nostalgic, esoteric, earlier sea poems. With very few exceptions, most of his other poetry, a wide if shallow river of verse, does not stand the test of time. *Sonnets and Poems* (1916), published when Masefield was at the height of his artistic power in the realm of verse narratives, is particularly interesting to students of Masefield for it shows in microcosm his contemporary strength and future weakness as a poet. Despite the praise the sonnets received, they are weak efforts. They read as if Masefield felt that he, like Spenser, Shakespeare, and Wordsworth before him, had to write the obligatory sonnet sequence.

A sonnet sequence is a very difficult objective for a poet to fulfill successfully which is why, despite the great number written, so few are still read. Such a sequence is so difficult because it essentially strikes a single note, one idea in one form; and the poet must be able to create variety and vitality within the most narrow range. Masefield's sonnet sequence with its "crooning cadences that describe his searchings for beauty do not escape monotony. Beauty becomes his favorite word, like Wit in Pope and God in Browning; and after many repetitions it loses its effulgence. The danger of this seeking after beauty is like that of too much seeking after religion."[1]

The beauty praised is, of course, not physical or personified in the form of a lovely girl; it is the concept or ideal of beauty that is so honored and revered. "Something of what Nature was to Wordsworth, Beauty is to Masefield—a healing influence, an inalienable treasure, an inspiration constantly invoked."[2] Despite the earthiness of much of his work, Masefield seems to consider the genteel verse he wrote as being, if not his best work, at least his most "artistic" efforts. A part of him cerebralized the role of poet as entwining life and art together in an Arthurian quest for beauty.

81

Naturally, the sonnets and much of the poetry in later volumes are concerned with the "truth" of existence; and this "truth" is manifested in comments and in opinions about the controversy between the ideas of evolutionary science and those of metaphysical belief. Thus the sonnets, unlike the narratives, are neo-Victorian and are closer by far in spirit to Tennyson than to T. S. Eliot. The poems debate the objective existence of a collective world-soul that is conjectured as beauty in phenomena, as well as the existence of the individual human soul that is manifested by the intuitive ability to perceive and appreciate that beauty.[3] Masefield was also struggling to determine if the intuition of beauty was created by external divine inspiration or if it was merely an illusion created in and by sensitive men through subconscious processes. The results are, of course, inconclusive.

I Three Fine Poems

The 1916 sonnets, despite Masefield's great scheme and good intention, are thus lifeless and uninspiring. In the volume, however, are three fine poems: "August, 1914," "The Wanderer," and "The River." The first is Masefield's best reflective poem, written upon receiving the news of the outbreak of war and of the mobilization of the British army. Like other artists who suddenly are made aware that their beautiful environs and their beloved homeland are about to undergo difficult times and irrevocable, undesirable change, Masefield was stirred to give poetic form and permanence to the beauty of a place that was soon to be awash with change, he wished to capture it in his own heart for his own recollection and inspiration and also to make an emotional picture for the edification and inspiration of Englishmen yet to come.

Masefield broods, for example, over the peaceful and lovely Berkshire valley:

> An endless quiet valley reaches out
> Past the blue hills into the evening sky;
> Over the stubble, cawing goes a rout
> Of rooks from harvest, flagging as they fly.
>
> So beautiful it is, I never saw
> So great a beauty on these English fields,
> Touched by the twilight's coming into awe,
> Ripe to the soul and rich with summer's yields.

He recalls the generations of men who have toiled to make the land productive and who, as Englishmen, have been ever ready to die

> . . . in foreign lands
> For some idea but dimly understood
> Of an English city never built by hands
> Which love of England prompted and made good.

Powerfully, one of the two or three true war images in this poem that preambles Britain's most terrible conflict, comes in the last line of the last stanza in order to tie together history, the presence of nature watching men, and the immediacy of war's destruction of both past and nature:

> And silence broods like spirit on the brae,
> A glimmering moon begins, the moonlight runs
> Over the grasses of the ancient way
> Rutted this morning by the passing guns.

It may have been an enthusiastic exaggeration to call "August, 1914" the best English poem of World War I,[4] but it surely is a very fine poem.

In terms of understanding his esthetics, "The Wanderer" is one of Masefield's most important poems. The ship, which he first saw as a boy aboard the *Conway*, was, as he said in the earlier poem, "Biography," a dominating influence on his inner and outward life. Besides appearing in the two poems, the vessel is used anonymously in the prose work, *A Tarpaulin Muster* (1907), and finally in *The Wanderer of Liverpool* (1930), a book of combined prose history and verse that relates the actual story of Masefield's symbol-vessel from her launching at Liverpool in 1860 to her loss in 1907 in the mouth of the Elbe River, Germany. As this narrative is the poet's historical catechism of his Art-Beauty symbol and as the poem "The Wanderer" is his verse prayer, the section in *A Tarpaulin Muster*, his fictional rendering of his hallmark symbol, is bedecked with perhaps unconscious sexual imagery:

When I saw her first there was a smoke of mist about her as high as her foreyard. Her topsails and flying kites had a faint glow upon them where the dawn caught them. Then the mist rolled away from her, so that we could see her hull and the glimmer of the red sidelight as it was hoisted inboard. She was rolling slightly, tracing an arc against the heaven, and as I

watched her the glow upon her deepened, till every sail she wore burned
rosily like an opal turned to the sun, like a fiery jewel. She was radiant, she
was of an immortal beauty, that swaying, delicate clipper. Coming as she
came, out of the mist into the dawn, she was like a spirit, like an intellectual
presence. Her hull glowed, her rails glowed; there was colour upon the
boats and tackling. She was a lofty ship (with skysails and royal staysails),
and it was wonderful to watch her, blushing in the sun, swaying and
curveting. She was alive with a more than mortal life. One thought that she
would speak in some strange language or break out into a music which
would express the sea and that great flower in the sky. She came trembling
down to us, rising up high and plunging; showing the red lead below her
water-line; then diving down till the smother bubbled over her hawseholes.
She bowed and curveted; the light caught the skylights on the poop; she
gleamed and sparkled; she shook the sea from her as she rose. There was no
man aboard of us but was filled with the beauty of that ship.[5]

"The Wanderer," a poem of seventy stanzas, begins with talk
about the beautiful ship, whose sailing the persona has regretfully
just missed. A storm arises; there is worry as to the safety of the
vessel; *The Wanderer* limps back to port, battered and bruised and
defeated by nature; but she is proud, glorious, and, above all,
beautiful in her suffering and defeat. Because she is now a jinxed
ship, a crew is mustered with difficulty; but she sails from Liverpool. The persona does not see her again for years until she is in a
southern port on a Christmas Eve when he is trying to understand
and relive his childhood. While he is struggling for the source and
the meaning of his life, suddenly, like inspiration from the oversoul,

> Old memories came: that inner prompting spoke.
> And bright above the hedge a seagull's wings
> Flashed and were steady upon empty air.
> "A Power unseen," I cried, "prepares these things;
> Those are her bells, the *Wanderer* is there."
>
> . . . .
>
> Even as my thought had told, I saw her plain;
> Tense, like a supple athlete with lean hips,
> Swiftness at pause, the *Wanderer* come again—
>
> Come as of old a queen, untouched by Time,
> Resting the beauty that no seas could tire,
> Sparkling, as though the midnight's rain were rime,
> Like a man's thought transfigured into fire.

The *Wanderer* is inspiration, the source of art and of what is best in human life. The majestic vessel has endured; it has survived and prevailed as life itself must and will. As Masefield states in the last line, "The meaning shows in the defeated thing," he once more expounds the theme that defeat may become victory through courage and perseverance. "All the essential Masefield is in this poem: his love of the sea and ships, of the countryside, and of the common man; his sympathy with 'the defeated thing;' his simple joy . . . And implicit throughout is his philosophy that beauty, glimpsed in moments of intense vision, is the revelation of something beyond itself. Here is the perfect utterance, fitting the perfect occasion."[6]

"The River," a shorter narrative, is the third particularly fine poem. In this story about a capsized ship and a sailor with infinite patience, who in disregard of the derision of those trapped with him, cuts his way out of the vessel's bottom and alone survives. An exciting and suspenseful tale, it teaches the moral lesson of endurance and self-reliance. The poem is starkly realistic; it combines Masefield's superb storytelling ability with his intimate knowledge of seamen.

II *Other Works*

Masefield's literary production at this time was so staggering that he must have written at the urging of a demon. *Lollingdon Downs* (1917) again contained sonnets, some sixty of them. They and the accompanying lyrics are more abstract, more thoughtful, and less interesting than his previous work. Action, Masefield's forte, has begun to disappear from his poetry and to blossom in his novels. Body and spirit are once more at war in his cerebral verse. The neo-Victorian again rises when his poetry is consciously "intellectual."

Other collections of verse soon followed. They include *The Cold Cotswolds* (1917); *The Dream* (1922); *Sonnets of Good Cheer* (1926); *Midsummer Night and Other Tales in Verse* (1928), a narrative collection from the Arthuriad in which Masefield blends traditional characterizations of Arthur, Lancelot, and Guinevere with the English countryside and the lovely passing of the seasons; and *South and East* (1929). None of these works added to Masefield's reputation. He was rapidly becoming the National Bard, but he was also moving further and further away from the main stream of current poetry. Still in high regard with the ever-diminishing popular poetry audience, he was losing critical support and many more discriminating readers. Although Masefield as Poet Laureate did not intend to write official verse celebrating royal births, deaths, anniversaries, and other occasions, he was turning out by 1935 many poems that commemorated events of public importance. Among his dutiful odes were poems to Queen Mary, George VI, Neville Chamberlain, Franklin Delano Roosevelt, and the young Princess Elizabeth. No more needs to be said concerning the damage that the laureateship did to a sensitive poet who had too much sense of duty.

More collections of verse followed, the most notable being *Minnie Maylow's Story* (1931), a collection of poems and scenes particularly about lovers like Tristan and Isolt; *On the Hill* (1949), poems of country things and ghosts; *The Bluebells* (1961), twenty-one landscape, seascape, and historical poems; *Old Raiger* (1965), twelve tales and reflective poems; and *In Glad Thanksgiving* (1966), reminiscences in verse and three long historical poems. Masefield's heart, however, was no longer in poetry as lyrical expression or as narrative. He turned his verse to autobiography, and his storytelling interest moved almost entirely into the area of fiction and then finally to the retelling of certain, select parts of his early life and experience. The requirements and adulation of the laureateship, faithfully pursued by an honest writer, had corrupted and destroyed the poet in John Masefield.

In a 1931 lecture, Masefield defined poetry as being of two kinds, a lesser and a greater:

> There is a lesser poetry, as we all know. There is that poetry given to the Messenger, who is not a clever nor a worthy man, who halts by the way, in taverns and marketplaces, listening to people, and at last delivers his message as one who has not understood it, all mixed with talk learned on the road.
>
> But the greater poetry is a flowing in of light from the source of all light, from that King from whom comes our knowledge of the kingly, in whose wisdom we advance, under whose majesty we move, and in whose beauty, if we have cared for beauty, we may come to dwell.[7]

In a way, Masefield was describing the paradox of his own poetry. Although he certainly was a worthy man and an intelligent one, he was most clearly a messenger. As a narrative poet, he played that role well. But, when he thought of himself as a Romantic poet inspired by spiritual beauty and wisdom rather than by the ways and the words of human beings, he failed to understand his own highest talent.

CHAPTER 5

Plays: A False Start

IN the preface to *The Collected Plays of John Masefield* (1919), the author says "I was a playwright, according to my powers, for ten years [1904-1914] during which the theatre in England was the main interest of my fellows and myself."[1] Masefield had become deeply interested in the drama because of his close friendship with Synge and Yeats, and he hoped that, like Synge, he could give to English drama a powerful folk idiom and that, like Yeats, he could create an archetypal Expressionist-Symbolist core as the latter had done for Irish drama. Masefield wrote several experimental one-act plays in verse and prose and four dramas which were well received critically in his time and which caused at least one reviewer of 1919 to deplore Masefield's decision to give up the English theater.[2]

Masefield's four important plays are *The Tragedy of Nan*, a three-act, prose folk tragedy in the style of Synge; *Pompey the Great*, a three-act, prose tragedy in the style of a Shakespearean Roman play; *The Faithful*, a three-act prose tragedy that is a derivative of Yeats' Symbolist drama and reminiscent of an Elizabethan play; and *Philip the King*, a long, one-act, rhymed verse drama in the tone of classical Greek tragedy. The first two plays had successful London productions as did some of the experimental one-act plays. Masefield had approached playwriting with reverence, and he set out in drama to write great literature. For him, a play was "a magnifying glass turned upon . . . the heart or brain or essence of life."[3]

Having read and studied deeply Greek tragedy and French Neoclassic drama, Masefield considered the unities of time, place, and action to be quite useful in drama.[4] This penchant for Classical form was one of his limitations as a dramatist, for Masefield approached drama essentially not as theater, a live performance for living people, but rather as Browning and Tennyson did; for to them drama was literature for the ages. In a way, more so than Sir Arthur Wing Pinero for example, Masefield was the last Victorian playwright.

A second limitation was Masefield's theory of tragedy that is implied in his criticism of other contemporary English dramatists: "Our playwrights have all the powers except that power of exultation which comes from delighted brooding on excessive, terrible things."[5] Great tragedy does not emerge from a static brooding on "excessive, terrible things." That is the business of the chorus, not the characters. Gory incidents do not necessarily prove emotional response for tragedy is a spiritual reaction to a human being's doomed confrontation with that which is best and worst in the universe or with that which is best and worst in himself. Furthermore, as one critic has pointed out, the word "excessive" is a giveaway: "It may be that the whole fault lies at bottom in that word *excessive*, whose legitimate offspring could hardly be other than pathetic and melodramatic."[6]

Lastly, although Masefield said that "a play is a contest between opposed wills, or a contest between a human will and the Fate which surrounds him,"[7] his dramatic conflict is always man against destiny. The elements of human confrontation between person and person as well as self-confrontation are lacking in his plays. But Masefield, who was, if anything, an honest man, overreacted when he summarized his career as a playwright: "I was attracted [to the theatre] by people like Granville Barker, Galsworthy and Yeats but I was never any good as a playwright."[8] Masefield was "dramatic," but in this respect he was like Browning; he had the ability to bring character to life through narrative. He could best achieve this feat as a narrative poet, the occupation he turned to immediately after giving up serious thoughts of a playwriting career. It was in the verse narrative that he found the medium for dramatic expression or, as he put it, found what he could do.

I The Tragedy of Nan

Masefield described the writing of *The Tragedy of Nan*, his most successful play, thus: "After I had finished *The Locked Chest*, I wished to try a longer play. A friend in London told me of a case of miscarriage of justice which had happened in Kent early in the last century. I took this as the groundwork of my fable for *The Tragedy of Nan*. I added some inventions to the fable, such as an unhappy love affair, and the characters of the household. I began the play in

January and finished it in September, 1907, at Greenwich"[9]; and it was produced by the Pioneers at the New Royalty Theatre on May 24, 1908, under the direction of Mr. Harley Granville-Barker. Set in rural western England, the landscape, as in a play by Synge, is itself a character in the drama; and Masefield, like an Elizabethan, uses language to paint the scenes and to establish character and mood through imagery and dialect. The intensity and the flair of the figurative speech are Irish although the words, are English when, for example, Nan says: "You'll listen to me. You 'ad me in your power. And wot was good in me you sneered at. And wot was sweet in me, you soured. And wot was bright in me you dulled. I was a fly in the spider's web. And the web came round me and round me, till it was a shroud, till there was no more joy in the world. Till my 'eart was bitter as that ink, and all choked. And for that I get little yellow round things [gold coins]." Masefield believed that he was capturing the spirit of the English country people through their own dialect. Some readers might object to Nan's and other characters' use of figurative imagery as being unrealistic or literary, but they would have had to object to Shakespeare's image usage as well as to the language of Irish playwrights like Synge, Yeats, and O'Casey.

Set in the house of a small tenant farmer on the banks of the Severn in 1810, the play, dedicated to William Butler Yeats, is the tragedy of Nan Hardwick, a lovely and gentle country girl whose father, as one later learns, has been unjustly hanged for the theft and killing of a single sheep. She has come to stay with her cousins, the Pargetters, who have a daughter, Jenny, who is neither as pretty nor as virtuous as Nan. In jealousy, Jenny causes her mother to make Nan's life miserable. Nan loves Dick Gurfil, a handsome but easily swayed young man; and, when he proposes to Nan, she accepts.

> DICK. My beautiful. I'll make a song for you, my beautiful.
> NAN. Your loving me, that's song enough.

Jenny, in her hatred of Nan, sets her cap for Dick. Dick surrenders to Jenny's argument that Nan, a murderer's daughter, is unfit for him; he proposes to Jenny, renounces his love for Nan, and heaps scorn upon her. Later, when government officials arrive to report "A sad miscarriage of justice," Nan is given fifty pounds in gold in compensation for her father. Now that "Miss Nan" is everyone's favorite, Dick tries to win her again. Instead, she stabs him for his infidelity and leaves to drown herself in the sea.

The plot is obviously melodramatic; but, like Hardy's *Tess of the D'Urbervilles*, Nan is a truly tragic figure, and the finest character in all of Masefield's drama. "Her natural incapacity for suspicion, her blindness to her lover's poorness of spirit, her own frank sanity of instinct, her gallant lavishness in affection, the touch of grandeur in her revenge, which to her is no mere wreaking of a private hate, but the rescue of other women from her own griefs—all this is unsurpassable. She stands out white and columnar from among the creeping things of the dark place she moves in."[10]

Dick Gurvil is also well drawn as the recreant lover, the weak-willed voluptuary, and the ever-present male chauvinist who feels that women are his for the taking. A third character worth noting is Gaffer Pearce, an old fiddler, who represents through his language, his song, and his stories the very spirit of the land. Like his model Synge, Masefield has a deep sympathy for his rural people. "He studies peasant cruelty without either raging at it, or idealizing it into something else, and he works it into his picture without brutalizing the picture's effect as a whole."[11]

II The Tragedy of Pompey the Great

Masefield described the writing of *Pompey the Great* thus: "When I was finishing *Nan* I worked at a one-act play upon *The Death of Pompey the Great*, as described in the life of Pompey in North's *Plutarch*. The tragedy of Pompey seemed to be too big a subject for a one-act play, so I left the draft and began anew on fuller lines. I wrote the first act of the play in 1908 in London and the second and third acts in 1909 at Great Hampden."[12] The play was produced by the Stage Society at the Aldwych Theatre, London, on December 4, 1910, under the direction of Mr. Harcourt Williams. Masefield's Pompey, like Shakespeare's Brutus, is a character of grandeur, honesty, and vacillation. He is opposed to democracy and believes that Ceasar will lead Rome to rule by the rabble. Nevertheless, Pompey, a tired but wise general, wishes peace rather than war. Pride and circumstance prevent compromise; and the war, as inevitable as the Trojan War in Giraudoux's *Tiger at the Gates*, is pursued until Pompey is defeated at Pharsalia and assassinated in Egypt. This play, written just a few years before World War I, seems to sense a coming conflict; for it is a great plea for peace and compromise, for the setting aside of pride, and for rational negotiation instead of emotional jingoism. But, in the play as in the world, compromise and reason fail.

Masefield says "War is terrible." When he wrote *Pompey the Great*, he did not yet really know how terrible it was.

The play is tightly constructed and shows that Masefield had mastered the craft of drama, if not the spirit. In keeping with the styles of his mentors, Synge and Shakespeare, the play contains passages of beautiful lyrical tenderness as when Pompey stands over the body of his young lieutenant, Flaccus, and says: "When you were born, women kissed you, and watched you as you slept, and prayed for you, as women do. When you learned to speak, they praised you; they laughed and were so tender with you, even when they were in pain. And to-night you will wander alone, where no woman's love can come to you, and no voice speak to you, and no grief of ours touch you to an answer. The dead must be very lonely."

Also of great beauty is the play's end. As Pompey is stabbed and as his wife Cornelia and Pompey's supporters sail away to the tune of a sea chanty, a choric sense of tragedy is evoked by a scene that is equal to the best in the Celtic Renaissance:

THE MATE. They stabbed him in the back.
ANTISTIA. It's ebb-tide now, my beauty.
THE CAPTAIN. (*yelling*) Cut the cable.
   Chopping forward.
A VOICE. All gone, the cable.
THE MATE. Let fall.
A VOICE. All gone.
THE MATE. Sheet home. Hoist away.
THE MEN. Ho.
   They haul.
THE CHANTYMAN. Away ho!
   The MEN haul.
   He intones in a clear loud voice. The Seamen sing the chorus, hauling.
   Their song is sung like an ordinary halliard chanty. The chorus is to the tune of the old chanty of "Hanging Johnny." The solo will be intoned clearly, without tune. It goes to fast time, the chorus starting almost before the soloist ends his line. The MEN must haul twice, in the proper manner, in each chorus.
THE CHANTYMAN.
Kneel to the beautiful women who bear us this strange brave fruit.
THE MEN. Away, i-oh.
THE CHANTYMAN.
Man with his soul so noble: man half god and half brute.
THE MEN. So away, i-oh.

THE CHANTYMAN.
Women bear him in pain that he may bring them tears.
CHORUS.
THE CHANTYMAN.
He is a king on earth, he rules for a term of years.
CHORUS.
THE CHANTYMAN.
And the conqueror's prize is dust and lost endeavour.
CHORUS.
THE CHANTYMAN.
And the beaten man becomes a story for ever.
CHORUS.
THE CHANTYMAN.
For the gods employ strange means to bring their will to be.
CHORUS.
THE CHANTYMAN.
We are in the wise gods' hands and more we cannot see.
CHORUS. So away, i-oh.
A VOICE. High enough.
THE MATE. Lie to. (*The Seamen lay to the fall.*) Make fast.
Coil up.
A VOICE. All clear to seaward.
THE CAPTAIN. Pipe down.
   The Bosun pipes the belay.
CURTAIN

But the play is marred by too much of a Dryden-like conscious
sense of classicism and melodramatic posing. Furthermore,
Masefield's theme of victory in defeat wears a little thin in this play
for it is difficult to see the triumph of Pompey's character as he loses
battles, the war, and Rome to Caesar and is then humiliated and
murdered. Although Masefield tries hard, he does not communicate
that essential paradox of tragedy: the tragic hero rises in moral
stature through suffering as he falls in material position to defeats.
Pompey is too much a paragon from first to last.

III   The Faithful

Masefield's drama had moved from early nineteenth-century
England to ancient Rome. Venturing even further afield, Masefield
turned in *The Faithful* to Japanese history as a source for his drama:

My next play was *The Faithful*, a pageant showing the tragedy of the 47
Ronin of Japan. This play was begun at Hampstead in January and finished

at Great Hampden in May, 1913. I had known the story of The Ronin for many years, and had long hoped to make a play of it, but could not see a dramatic form for it. I planned it and began to write it (in 1912) as a tale in verse, but changed my mind on seeing Mr. Granville Barker's productions of *Twelfth Night* and *The Winter's Tale*. They shewed me more clearly than any stage productions known to me the power and sweep of Shakespeare's construction of "scene undivided and passion unlimited." They helped me to construct *The Faithful* as a play with "continuous performance" for a double or platform stage.[13]

This more experimental play was first performed at the Birmingham Repertory Theatre on December 4, 1914. After the war, the play had a respectable New York run of forty-nine performances at the Garrick Theatre where it opened on October 13, 1919. Although well received critically for the most part, the play was never considered a "commercial property" like *The Tragedy of Nan* or *Pompey the Great*.

In the play, Kira, who once ate "broken meats after the feast" and who has now risen quickly in life to become a Daimyo and rich, brings about the death of the good young leader Asano. In the ensuing conflict, the followers of Asano are routed and their property seized. Those who try to avenge Asano also have terrible things happen to them: their parents and their wives commit suicide; their children either kill themselves or starve to death. Finally, after a year's ordeal, the revengers under the command of Asano's friend Kurano, succeed, and Kira is slain. The play ends with the satisfied victims about to kill themselves in accordance with the sentence that the law has passed upon them.

The play is almost a ritual, for the moments of killing are highly formal. Since the play grows more and more remote and contrived, Masefield's drama becomes more "poetic" and less dramatic. Somehow, the action he was able to inject into his verse narratives began to escape him because of the growing rhetorical direction of his plays. *The Faithful* has, of course, some superb lyric moments as when, at the end of Act I, Asano, about to die, says:

> Sometimes, in wintry springs,
> Frost on a midnight breath,
> Comes to the cherry flowers
> And blasts their prime;
> So I, with all my powers
> Unused on men or things,
> Go down the wind to death,
> And know no fruiting-time.

In another moment Kurano, pretending to be mad drunk in the hope that the villainous Kira will not watch him too closely, speaks in Hamlet-like melancholy: "Sometimes I am sad, for all my merry-making. It is not such an easy world. There is a fellow, Death, who is a danger, if one could find him. I had a friend once; my head is all in a whirl; a very dear friend: I could weep when I think what happened to him."

A scene between Kurano and his son Chikara, which occurs just as the revengers are about to execute Kira, is particularly poignant. Kurano says: "Once a woman of our ancestors was defending a doorway with her husband against the enemy. She was shot in the breast with an arrow. She cried to her husband, 'Never mind me. But use my body as a shield and keep the door.' So he did." "Was she killed, father?" Chikara asks, and Kurano answers: "As far as such souls die she died." In this scene, when Kurano knows that he and his son are soon to die, he takes leave of life indirectly by speaking of his dead wife. Kurano: "If we see Kira, if we get near him, keep my left side and back." Chikara: "I will, father, while I live." Kurano: "You are like your mother, boy. She was a very noble woman, Chikara. She told me strange things, once, long ago. Come, now. Sing as we go lad." "All the evil in the world," Kurano tells his son, "is at the mercy of a word." *The Faithful* contains an unforgettable hero, Kurano, who is so faithful to the memory of his dead friend. As in an Elizabethan revenge play like *The Revenger's Tragedy*, revenge itself becomes the purpose and the passion of the hero's life. As in the revenge play, there is a call for revenge, madness, and death. In a way, Masefield's superimposing a Japanese story on an Elizabethan stage concept—for the play is set on a platform stage with an inner room representing a room in a Japanese palace—is akin to the Japanese film director Kirusawa's interpreting *Macbeth* in a Japanese medieval setting in *Throne of Blood*. But theater is not film, and Masefield's "Japan" does not achieve credibility. All in all, *The Faithful* is interesting, is ahead of its time, but is still a highly synthetic drama.

IV   Philip the King

Masefield "began the verse play, in one act, of *Philip the King*, about January, 1914 . . . . at Hampstead."[14] After he had finished it in May, it was first performed at Covent Garden Theatre in London on November 5, 1914. However, *Philip the King* is more of a dramatic poem than a play, for it is almost devoid of action. In the story, Philip of Spain is waiting for news of the Spanish Armada;

and he is full of confidence and pride. When his daughter the Princess expresses fear that the enterprise might fail, Philip is confident that God, whose instrument he believes himself to be, will not fail the Spanish cause. When Philip falls asleep over his papers, spirits enter one at a time. They are ghosts of Indian slaves and of Europeans of the recent historical past whom Philip has betrayed. They torment Philip who believes them to be spirits of evil.

An English prisoner is brought to Philip, and he tells the King what he wants to hear: the Spanish have been victorious. Philip is overjoyed, and he and the Church prepare to celebrate the victory. Finally survivors of the Armada enter with inklings of the truth and a messenger arrives with the whole story of the defeat of the Armada: "Philip, your Navy is beneath the waves." The messenger then tells the entire tale in some two hundred and fifty lines of very good narrative verse that is broken only by an occasional interjection from Philip. The description of the battle is quite fine, but it is not theater. The play ends with Philip's hoping to "Set out another fleet against that land" as he, in his misery, kneels to pray.

Masefield has attempted to construct Philip as a Greek tragic hero; he is destroyed by his own blind pride; for, serving evil, he thinks that he is serving good. Masefield's use of the messenger, the long dialogue of Philip with his daughter, and the mixture of rhymed and unrhymed verse with passages of prose, are reminiscent of the Attic mode; but the play fails as Greek tragedy because the perspective is English and not Spanish. The audience does not suffer with Spanish Philip, the victim of hubris; it rejoices with England, the survivor of the evil.

V   Other Plays

During Masefield's ten-year dramatic interlude, he wrote several other one-act plays including *The Campden Wonder* (1905-1906), *Mrs. Harrison* (1906), *The Sweeps of Ninety-Eight* (1906), *The Locked Chest* (1906), and lastly *Good Friday*, which was begun in 1914 with high hopes, and much reworked by Masefield. Performed in 1917, it survives as a dramatic poem rather than as a play. Later Masefield would write other dramas such as *Melloney Holtspur* (1922), *A King's Daughter* (1922), *The Trial of Jesus* (1925), *Tristan and Isolt* (1927), *End and Beginning* (1934), and *A Play of St. George* (1948). When Masefield translated and adapted Racine's *Esther* and *Berenice* in 1922, he found the French playwright's Neo-classical values and his use of poetry quite sympathetic.

After 1918, however, Masefield no longer considered himself as a writer for the professional theater. He built his own little theater at his home near Oxford and had his own company, the Boar's Hill Players, perform there and sometimes in the college halls of Oxford. His company played Masefield's new drama, *The Trial of Jesus*, and the experimental works of other, younger poet-playwrights during the period between the two world wars.

John Masefield's dramatic values were Classical, his intentions Shakespearean, and his training that for a playwright of the Celtic Renaissance. He wrote plays as if he had never heard of Ibsen, Strindberg, Karl Marx, or the Industrial Revolution. If, as a poet, he was a great Georgian, as a playwright he was a mediocre Victorian. If he had studied the theater more and had applied some of the courage and innovation of his verse narratives to his dramatic endeavors, Masefield's contribution to the English stage might possibly have been more memorable. As it is, the best parts of his plays are lyrical passages of superb poetry, never moments of dramatic action.

If playwriting was a false start for Masefield, it nevertheless had some good effects. For one, the success of *The Tragedy of Nan* helped to establish his reputation as a writer. More important, however, the discipline of the playwright's craft in respect to plot and character offered Masefield a training in focus which served him in good stead as a novelist. His natural talent as a poet for description and his experiences in life also contributed to his success as a novelist. His characters in his novels would never be vague; and his plots, although sometimes improbable, were never disjointed.

CHAPTER 6

Storytelling in Prose: The Novels

WITH everything else he did, John Masefield also wrote twenty-two novels. Six of them were for young people: *A Book of Discoveries* (1910), *Martin Hyde* (1910), *Lost Endeavor* (1910), *Jim Davis* (1911), *The Midnight Folk* (1927), and *A Box of Delights* (1935). The sixteen adult novels represent an enormous range of skill, subject, locale, period, style, and even chronology; for Masefield was an active, publishing novelist from 1908 to 1947. If he had not first made his reputation as a poet, if he had not become Poet Laureate just when he had turned most fully to the writing of novels, and if he had not written so unevenly, Masefield might have been taken seriously as a novelist. For it must be acknowledged at the outset of any study of Masefield the novelist that his work in this genre, although often delightful and frequently profound, is occasionally embarrassingly bad. As in his poetry, his exquisitely wrought sequences can be followed by surprising lapses of structure or of imagination.

Masefield's adult novels are best considered in thematic groups. First of all, there are the sea novels which represent his earliest, most popular, and best work: *Captain Margaret* (1908), *The Bird of Dawning* (1933), and *Victorious Troy: or, The Hurrying Angel* (1935). In the second most significant group are the Conrad-like novels of Latin America and Africa: *Multitude and Solitude* (1909), *Sard Harker* (1924), *ODTAA* (1926), *The Taking of the Gry* (1934), and *Dead Ned* (1938) when considered with its sequel, *Live and Kicking Ned* (1939). Third are the Thomas Hardy-Arnold Bennett-like novels of life in nineteenth- and early twentieth-century England: *The Street of To-day* (1911), *The Hawbucks* (1929), *Eggs and Baker* (1936), and *The Square Peg* (1937). Last in importance, achievement, and incidentally in order of writing are the medieval novels; *Basilissa* (1940) and *Conquer* (1941), which are set in the

98

Byzantium of Justinian and Theodora; and *Badon Parchments* (1947), which is located in the ancient Britain of King Arthur.

Although Masefield continued to write verse narratives, albeit shorter ones, after *King Cole*, it was primarily in the realm of the novel that he chose to continue his role as a storyteller. As a novelist, even more so than as a narrative poet, the primary motivation which drove Masefield to pen and paper was his ever-deepening desire to give pleasure to his fellow human beings. The basic ingredients of his novels were his sea experiences and his affection for his country—especially its rural past—and also his sharply honed sense of moral values. The great strengths of his novels are their strong plots and, particularly in the sea books, the verisimilitude of mood and setting. Perhaps the single most apparent weakness is the almost embarrassed straining of the occasional love story (Conrad had difficulty in that area, too) along with the resultant problems in drawing female characters. It is no coincidence that perhaps the two best Masefield novels, *The Bird of Dawning* and *Victorious Troy*, are set at sea and are devoid of women. Ultimately, "John Masefield's achievements in fiction are a poet's. He uses words with the utmost sensitivity. He occupies himself, and engages the reader in the minutiae of every phenomenon he undertakes to write about. . . ."[1]

I *The Sea*

Masefield's first novel is naturally a work about the sea, but *Captain Margaret* is also a love story and an historical romance. Basically, it is a well-plotted and entertaining yarn that is reminiscent of the work of Robert Louis Stevenson. Charles Margaret is a young English gentleman of the colonial period; some forty years old, he is handsome, romantic, and chivalric almost to a fault. He owns the sloop *Broken Heart*, so named because of Margaret's disappointment in his love for the beautiful Olivia. Along with his friend Ned Perrin and his sailing captain, a tough ex-pirate named Cammock, Margaret prepares to set sail on an expedition to the Spanish Main to free enslaved Indians from Spanish rule.

Margaret goes to Olivia (now married to a criminal named Stukeley whose evil nature she refuses to recognize) to pay farewell respects. Stukeley, who is again in trouble with the law, beguiles his not-too-bright wife into believing that he too would like to aid the poor Indians; and she convinces Margaret to allow both of them to sail with the *Broken Heart*. Margaret and all on board realize what a villain Stukeley is; but, because they are chivalrous, they do not enlighten Olivia about the true nature of her husband's character even when he disrupts shipboard life, seduces Olivia's not-too-reluctant maid, and finally deserts to the Spanish enemy.

When Captain Margaret and his allies capture a Spanish town in the West Indies, Masefield's description of the capture of the town and of its later unauthorized sacking is based on his research for the writing of his history *On the Spanish Main* (1906). This section of the novel is Masefield at his best with action. A small passage from the battle scene illustrates his ability to write exciting, evocative prose at this early time in his career:

There came cries and a noise of running. A few heads showed. The wall spouted fire in a volley. They were up against the wall, against the iron-plated door, piling the kegs against the hinges, tamping them down with sods and stones. Margaret snatched one keg and spilled it along the door-sill. "There," he said, "There. Now your fuse, fuseman." The quick-match was thrust into a keg. "Up along the walls, boys. Quick. Scatter. Pronto." He thrust them sideways. They saw what he wanted. When the im-aginations are alert there is little need for speech. No man could have heard him. The racket in the town was uproar like earthquake. The whole wall above them was lit with fire spurts. Mud and plaster were tinkling in a rain upon them. They ran fifty yards like hares, paying out the quick-match. "Now," said Margaret. The match flashed. A snake of fire rippled from them. They saw the shards of pots gleam, then vanish. They saw old bones, old kettles, all the refuse below the walls. "Down," he shouted. "Down." They flung themselves down. The beach to their left flashed, as the pirates fired at the wall.

There came a roar, a rush of fire, a shaking of the land. Mud, brick, stone, shards of iron and wood, all the ruin of the gate, crashed among them, flying far among the trees, thumping them on their backs as they lay. After the roar there was a dismayed silence. A wail of a hurt man sounded, as though the wrecked gate cried. Then with a volley the privateers stormed in. (330).

At the end, Stukeley is found dead in the ruins of the siege; and Olivia and Margaret will return to England to marry and to live happily ever after.

In *A Mainsail Haul* (1905) and *A Tarpaulin Muster* (1907), Masefield had put together fine collections of short stories and prose sketches in which he had tried a variety of styles and thematic ideas. The success of this work, particularly of *A Tarpaulin Muster*, showed the young author that he could write fiction and thus a venture into a long prose narrative was in order. *Captain Margaret* resulted, and its reception was encouraging enough for Masefield to continue in the genre.

The Bird of Dawning and *Victorious Troy*, which were written more than twenty-five years later, represent Masefield at the height of his ability as a novelist. Both books are about young men and ships, not about young men and young women; for in Masefield's novels, as G. Wilson Knight points out, "Ships, often regarded as living creatures, have the grace and beauty men usually attribute to women, whose place they fill in Masefield's narratives. . . ."[2] These two novels are brimful with the romance of the sailing ship. The reader can almost taste and feel the salt spray of the sea; his ears echo with the crack of spars, the creak of pulleys, and the groan of straining rope; and the two novels are alive with salty characters. The poet and the sailor and the novelist come together in these stories with a felicity that is nowhere else as evident in English or American literature except in the work of Conrad and Melville. Only those two sailor-writers equally command with Masefield the knowledge of the sea and the details of shipboard life.

The Bird of Dawning is the story of a sailing-ship race between clippers in the China tea trade in the last part of the nineteenth century. A twenty-four-year-old man who is studying for his mate's license finds himself in command of a lifeboat and a group of fellow seamen after their vessel has been rammed and sunk during a fog. After several days in an open boat, they come across an inexplicably deserted clipper. The young, but well-trained Englishman, whose name is Cyril (Cruiser) Trewsbury, is indeed true and equal to the task in front of him. A born leader, he inspires his crew to sail the deserted clipper to the English Channel and to victory in the race. In this very good yarn, Masefield's characterization is at its best, for each sailor begins to emerge as a separate and distinct human being after the sinking of their first vessel, the *Blackgauntlet*, and their testing on slim rations in an open lifeboat on a dangerous sea.

The storm scenes in *The Bird of Dawning* are perhaps even better than Conrads.'[3]

He had a little while to take stock of her, this little, crowded, eighteen foot boat, finding a way somehow in the toppling and confusion of wastes of water: going up, up, up, seething in a smother, pausing, rushing down a gliddering hill, with spray drenching down over their shoulders, then pausing again, sliding, edging, as it seemed, to one side or another, then trying it again, going on up the hill ahead. The swoops, and the hiss and rush and power of the great waves made his heart stand still at times, then the pluck and the cheek of the boat reassured him; and the vitality of the wind took hold of him till he felt confident, that he would bring his command through. (73)

Some of the seascapes are breathtaking paintings in prose:

> The ship was coming down on a soldier's wind under a press of canvas. Her royal masts had been sent down, probably in the storm of the night before, but she carried full topgallants and her fore topmast studdingsail. She was making probably twelve miles an hour in what seemed a succession of staggering pauses followed by lifting thrusts forward. She seemed to bow down till her bowsprit was deep in smother and her eyes submerged, then after a check amid the bubble she would rise and rise and clear what seemed like half her length all shaking with running water and surge herself forward still rising and rolling till the power of her fabric bowed down again. (152)

The Bird of Dawning is an almost totally successful work because the author has achieved in it just about everything he intended to do. Masefield desired to write a sailing chronicle, a frank adventure, and an engrossing, uncomplicated yarn; and he achieved these goals superbly.

Victorious Troy; or The Hurrying Angel is every bit the equal of *The Bird of Dawning*. The *Hurrying Angel*, a full rigged ship that is participating in the grain race of 1922, is hit by a cyclone in the South Pacific. On board is an eighteen-year-old senior apprentice named Dick Pomfret who is first seen as another happy boy who lives in the deck house with the other ship apprentices. He has no idea what life shortly will ask of him; but, as an English trained sea officer-to-be, he is unconsciously ready for any vicissitude. Indeed, the thought sometimes occurs to the reader of Masefield's novels that the sea was England's first colony.

Because the captain, an older generation bounder, gets drunk as the cyclone approaches, he fails to order adequate precautions and a safe course in the storm. The ship is struck as if by an artillery barrage, her masts go by the board, the senior officers are lost, and Captain Robin Battler Cobb is seriously disabled. In the midst of chaos and destruction, Dick gathers his wits, takes command, and painstakingly brings men and ship about to return to safety and to life. In the process, Dick Pomfret passes into manhood; the lost ship is saved; once more defeat is victory; and the analogy of the title with the epic of Troy becomes clear.

In 1922, the day of the commercial sailing vessel was nearly over. The depredations of submarine warfare in World War I and the economy and reliability of steam propulsion had all but eliminated the trade of sail, except for coastal schooners and a handful of square rigged movers of bulk cargo such as grain or coal. *Victorious Troy* is Masefield's artistic farewell to the vessels and to the seaways of his youth. Toward the end of the book, the *Hurrying Angel*, underway, but still looking like a wreck and in need of medical aid for the captain, is seen by a thirty-thousand-ton cruise ship. Suddenly the reader sees the anachronistic little vessel with modern eyes as the passengers crowd the steamship's rail and gaze through binoculars at the *Hurrying Angel* with amazement and bewilderment: "She stayed there, bowing easily into the swell, while all the hundreds of her pleasure-seekers flocked to her rail to stare. They did not understand what had happened to this little, shabby, battered ship, so salt-caked and rusty. They did not know the kind of ship, nor that sort of experience. They felt, somehow, that at last they were looking at the sea, about which they had so often read"(268). Two young men, first-class passengers on the liner, ask Dick to be taken on the *Hurrying Angel* as new hands because they want the experience and the trial of bringing a sailing ship home to England. For deep-sea sailing has become a trial of manhood rather than a means of livelihood.

As in *The Bird of Dawning,* the characterization here is excellent. The seaman types are all familiar to the ex-sailor Masefield. Each character develops through the action and the stress of events: the young apprentice lads like Kit Pillows, Ed Newbarn, and Bill Guller; the old salts, traditional English seamen like the veteran Bill Purple, Nab Wallers, and Burt Kempler; and, of course, the villains with their "foreign sounding" names—Kruger Evesbatch, and Morritz. Above all is Dick, who is finely drawn and, like Masefield himself, a *Conway*-trained apprentice officer.

Again the storm scenes and ships' descriptions are excellent:

Loach, the sideways man, was in the main rigging close by, stopping-up coils of gear out of the way. Dick saw that he needed a hand, so hopped up into the shrouds beside him and held up the coils while Loach secured them.

"Coming on pretty hard," he called.

The sideways man looked sideways and said:

"Powdered brick."

"Does it remind you of the war?" Dick asked.

The sideways man looked at Dick sideways, then at the weather sideways, and then said sideways to nobody:

"Like over a village in a barrage . . . all powdered brick. The war to end war. A General's idea of beauty."

Loach had spoken from what he had seen. Dick felt that he had described the case exactly. It was as though millions of red bricks had been blown to fine powder and then sprayed so as to cover heaven. Under this murk, which yet had a glare to it, the sea was rising irregularly with a snap and a snarl in a jagged unusual way, with the waves running into peaks, not into combs, and being slashed or plucked off and then flung down by what seemed like the act of invisible devils. (51-52)

In *The Bird of Dawning* and in *Victorious Troy*, as in other of his novels, Masefield does not use chapter divisions. The stories, like the sea itself, run on from cover to cover and from coast to coast. As long as men sail by wind, for pleasure if not for profit, these two novels will be read.

II *Latin America and Africa*

Of the six novels set in or concerned with Latin America, only the first one, *Multitude and Solitude*, deals in a truly realistic way with a faraway place. *Sard Harker*, *ODTAA*, and *The Taking of the Gry* are located in the Latin American republic of Santa Barbara which Masefield created for the purposes of his fiction just as Conrad created Costaguana for *Nostromo;* and the Africa referred to in *Dead Ned* and visited in *Live and Kicking Ned* is an Erehwon partially inhabited by a white race of men who are possibly descended from the ancient Greeks. Of these six novels, the Santa Barbara trilogy are the most skillfully wrought and the most interesting to read, for the country of Santa Barbara develops into a microcosm of nations, and a place which, transcending the individual novels, remains in the minds of readers.

Multitude and Solitude suggests in its title the contrasting impulses of a young man, Roger Naldrett, toward city life amidst the multitude of people and the solitude of service to science and humanity in Africa. Roger is a dramatist whose *magnum opus*, because of its somewhat advanced view of morals in its era, is booed off the stage. It is interesting to note that Masefield and his best friend, Synge, were both writing plays at this moment in their lives and that the reception of Roger's play in the novel is reminiscent of that received in Dublin by Synge's *The Playboy of the Western World.*

Bruised and in need of reassurance, Roger sails to Ireland to be with the Irish girl he loves, only to discover that she had drowned in a Channel accident. Distraught over the double blows to his equilibrium, Roger impulsively joins in a scientific expedition that is going to Central Africa to study sleeping sickness in the tropics. Roger is happy to be away from the narrow literary and artistic world of London, but the expedition meets with calamity as one by one the participants fall victim to the disease. When Roger discovers the antitoxin and saves everyone's life, including his own, he regains faith in himself and meaning in his life.

The novel contains appropriate social indignations for its time, and countless uninteresting pages deal with sleeping sickness and the tsetse fly. Along with every other of his preoccupations, Masefield continued to have a deep interest in medicine which was finally assuaged when he worked with the British Red Cross in World War I.

Multitude and Solitude seems strikingly autobiographical in retrospect, especially in comparison with the romance, *Captain Margaret* that was written just before it. A fair second novel, reasonably well crafted and interesting, it lacks a love story, as Roger's lover is conveniently killed off stage; but this is an advantage in the canon of Masefield's novels as the author could never be fully comfortable with love scenes.

For Gilbert Highet, Masefield's novels of Latin America "are in the same line as Stevenson's *Treasure Island*—only better, richer, more adult."[4] *Sard Harker* was written first and, critically speaking, it was the best received of his Latin American novels; it established Masefield's reputation as a novelist. In *Sard Harker* Masefield depicts the rough life and thoroughly enjoys spinning a yarn of ships, the sea, the jungle, icy mountains, burning deserts, political intrigue and lust in his mythical tropical republic of Santa Barbara and the states which border on it and which he called the "Sugar States." Masefield went so far as to draw maps of the "area" and to create a political and economic history for it.[5]

He wanted all three of the Latin American novels to appear to be emerging from a believable historical continuity and destiny. *Sard Harker* actually deals with later historical events than those in

ODTAA, and *The Taking of the Gry* follows both. The events of *Sard Harker* take place in 1897, ten years after the reign of terror of Santa Barbara's dictator, Don Lopez, has finally been brought to an end (the business of *ODTAA*). *The Taking of the Gry* is concerned with a revolution in Santa Barbara's neighbor, Santa Ana, in 1911.

Sard Harker is the mate of a fine clipper ship, the *Pathfinder*. Ten years before, he helped to save Don Manuel, the present dictator of Santa Barbara, from the clutches of Don Lopez. Sard is haunted by the beautiful face of a girl he once saw briefly in England and now dreams about. Because of her, Sard begins a cross-country journey that becomes a terrible nightmare of dreadful suffering that includes the crossing of a desert and a mountain range. When Sard locates the girl, Margarita, they fall into the clutches of a demonic mystic who has been the perpetrator of all the evil in the area. Sard struggles manfully, but it appears that he will be sacrificed and that Margarita will be ravished. At the last moment, however, they are rescued by Don Manuel, and the evil is expunged from the land. The book has many improbable accidents and a cliff-hanging, melodramatic ending, but the narrative is always engrossing, largely because of Sard's tortured endurance. The lush yet precise descriptions of tropics, mountains, and deserts shows that Masefield can successfully deal with these aspects of nature as well as with the sea.

Yet another young Englishman, the eighteen-year-old Highworth Foliat Ridden, is the hero of *ODTAA*. Fortunately, he is usually referred to as "Hi," and speaking of odd names, *ODTAA* stands for "one damned thing after another." Hi, who has come to Santa Barbara at his father's insistence to make his way in the world, arrives at a bad time because of the rebellion in the land. The Whites, a political party, are rising in arms against Don Lopez, the dictator and leader of the Reds. Carlotta, the beautiful heroine and the White leader, is taken by the Reds after she has captured Hi's heart. He plunges into the jungle and through the mountains on a Sard-Harker-like ordeal in order to bring a message to Carlotta's fiance, Don Manuel, who assumes the leadership of the inevitably successful White cause. The time is 1886 - 1887, and this Don Manuel rescues Sard Harker in his story ten years later.

Carlotta cannot be saved but, although she is put to death by Don Lopez, she becomes a martyr and her death a rallying point for the subsequent overthrow of Don Lopez. The young English hero, who is captured by the Reds and imprisoned with other foreign nationals in a Santa Barbara church, is evacuated on a British vessel.

Years later he returns to the war-stricken country and participates in its reorganization and recovery. Hi, like Sard before him, grows to manhood because of his trial by ordeal. He has witnessed beauty; he has done everything in his power to save it; the memory of it will stay with him and guide him throughout his life. This testing and proving of a young man against nature or against evil men is a recurring theme, almost a *sine qua non* in Masefield's novels. Masefield seems to recast and relive an idealization of his own youthful adventures. By implication, an initiation quest in a non-civilized environment precedes full admittance to the status of manhood in the civilized English tribe.

ODTAA is somewhat less successful than *Sard Harker;* for, stirring and exciting though it is, the book is somewhat marred by the author's straining over Santa Barbara's history in rambling summarizations and by a conclusion done in jerks and starts by means of notes, letters, and poems. Also the reader begins to sense that all this history, all this creation of an elaborate political situation and an evolving social order, is simply not going to lead to anything very profound. In all fairness to Masefield, he never states anywhere that his novels are designed in part as allegories of political morality. However, if telling the pleasing tale is all, then the reader can do with more telling and less historical exposition; for the structure of the Latin American trilogy, especially *ODTAA*, is weakened by the emergence of the bare and pointy bones of the saga of Santa Barbara and its neighboring state Santa Ana.

The Taking of the Gry deals with the revolution in Santa Ana of 1911 when that country successfully resisted annexation by its more powerful neighbor, Santa Barbara, which was aided by traitorous collaborators within Santa Ana. It has two heroes, both daredevil young men: Charles Tarlton, a British officer on a mail packet, who tells the story; and Lieutenant Tom Browne, who is of English descent, of the Santa Ana Navy. Tom is concerned that the president of Santa Ana is perfidiously about to turn over the country to Santa Barbara. Only the Santa Ana Navy is ready and willing to resist this aggression. After Tom has enlisted the aid of Charles, they plan to capture an ammunition ship in the harbor of Santa Barbara; and, by sailing it through a dangerous unused channel, called Drake's Channel, they wish to avoid recapture and turn the vessel over to Tom's party in Santa Ana. The munitions are enough to tilt the armament scale in favor of Tom's Nationalists. The ammunition ship is the *Gry*, a vessel with a carved horsehead as figurehead.

Once more young men endure and win through. Drake's Channel is an obvious and valid symbol; for, named after its discoverer, Sir Francis Drake, it symbolically represents the English way of fighting through difficulty for a just cause, to a moral end. Without women in central positions and without a love story in the book, Masefield is much more comfortable than in *Sard Harker* or in *ODTAA*. Structurally, *The Taking of the Gry* approaches the neatness and integrity of *The Bird of Dawning* and *Victorious Troy*. Shorter in length by some two hundred pages than *Sard Harker* and *ODTAA*, *The Taking of the Gry* is a compact and contained tale. It is an optimistic, buoyant narrative more like the work of Richard Harding Davis and Jack London than of such English adventure writers as Kipling and Stevenson. Again a work without profundity, its virtues are its vices: simplicity and directness.

All in all, the Latin American novels of John Masefield succeed more than they fail. They are engrossing stories. Readers do begin to believe in the existence of the Sugar States; and, though a search for the allegorical meaning of all this political creation leaves the reader still in the dark, he is able to recognize and appreciate Masefield's love of youth and his belief in its power to overcome. Endurance and overcoming, so peculiarly English, are as much the hallmarks of these Latin American novels as of other of Masefield's fiction and nonfiction.

The last two exotic adventure novels of John Masefield, *Dead Ned* and *Live and Kicking Ned*, must be considered together for they are two halves of a single story and the author must surely have planned from the beginning that the adventures of that young doctor, Edward (Ned) Mansell, would be spun out in two volumes or even three. The 289 pages of *Dead Ned* pose all the problems; for, as with other Masefield novels, this work is without chapter divisions. *Live and Kicking Ned*, in which the problems are resolved, is actually two separate novels in sequence, *Live Ned*, (253 pages long), and then, starting again with page one, *Kicking Ned*, (224 more pages). Neither of these two novels is divided into chapters or parts. Thus Ned has three divisions to his story, Dead, Live, and Kicking; and, if there is ever another edition of his tale, it should all be told between one pair of boards.

Muriel Spark considers *Dead Ned* to be Masefield's "best prose work" and "the peak of the poet's achievement in fiction."[6] Other critics might not agree, but surely the Ned stories, undertaken some four years after *Victorious Troy*, find Masefield still near the height of his prose narrative powers and unburdened by an artificial history or by conflicts between social classes.

The subtitle of *Dead Ned* is *The Autobiography of a Corpse*, for Dr. Mansell is hanged and revived in the story. Masefield was inspired to begin this story by a legend he was told while dining in the hall of the Guild of Barbers. The guildsmen told Masefield that it was once the custom to bring the corpses of hanged criminals from Tyburn Gallows to the Guildhall to be dissected by surgeon-barbers. The compassionate company of barber-surgeons had secretly agreed that if any hanged man or woman were not quite dead they would make every effort to bring the body back to life and help that person to escape because the law would surely demand the reexecution of that wretched person. "The Worshipful Company of Barbers maintain a legend to this day that a screen in their possession was sent to them by a grateful resurrected man, one of those who had been smuggled out of the country."[7]

Ned tells his own story. He is an eighteenth-century Londoner who has just finished his medical training and is about to start a promising career. Unfortunately, his father, a distinguished physician, has remarried; and Ned's stepmother is a cruel, stupid woman who has a profligate son. In the course of coming to know his new relatives, who immediately despise him, Ned befriends an eccentric, old, retired admiral who lives in Hannibal House that is named after his most famous command, and that is reputedly stuffed with hidden gold.

When the admiral is murdered, Ned is accused of the crime; sent to Newgate Prison, where Masefield gets in some memorable descriptions of that place of despair; is hanged; and is then revived in secret by a physician friend. Ned barely escapes pursuit on a slave ship bound to the coast of Africa, about which he has learned much from the murdered admiral. *Dead Ned*, which ends here, is particularly successful in its reconstruction of eighteenth-century London life and the rural surroundings of that city. The characterizations are memorable, for Ned is a living character whose death and resurrection are absolutely believable. The cranky old salt of an admiral is especially well drawn, as are several of the minor figures. Above all, the book is pervaded with a dark, brooding sense of melancholy, horror, and evil; and Ned's hanging becomes not only the great trauma of his life but also the universal tone and mood-setting trauma of the world of both books. Since *Dead Ned* snaps off the story at a high point, the reader wonders if

Ned will survive the new dangers in his life, if he will be able to prove his innocence eventually, and if the real murderer of Admiral Topsle Kringle will be discovered.

Dead Ned, unlike *Live and Kicking Ned,* not only has a distinct eighteenth-century flavor to it but is almost an eighteenth-century novel itself in respect to plot, characterization, and even writing style. An example is Ned's description of his first meeting with his pretentious and vain stepmother:

> My father was almost without that vanity; he showed it only in trifles in his dress. My stepmother had it to the full. She had the languor, as though she were too exquisite a plant to live in such loutish air, having once breathed at Versailles or at St. Cloud. She had the manner, as one who has seen a play may affect the manner of a player. She had the dress, of one who would buy what she was sold.
>
> There she lay languishing on her sofa, with her eyes half-closed, and her white, plump, and rather useless hand plying a fan. She smiled on my appearance and held her left hand idly to me. She did not rise. I think that she meant me to kiss the outstretched hand. I shook it, instead, and saw her compress her lips with disdain as she said in French that his young *étourdi* was wanting in manner at present and smacked too much of the apothecary. I knew French rather better than she, as it chanced, but I said nothing, then. (16 - 17)

Live and Kicking Ned continues the young doctor's story as he is on his way to Africa aboard the slave ship. The plot grows fantastical. Ned treats and befriends ill slaves as a physician should do and is spared a horrible death by avenging blacks. He makes his way into the interior and comes upon a civilization of whites surrounded by black Africans. The white Kranois have a highly civilized city reminiscent of Troy or Athens or even Constantinople and it is even suggested that the Kranois are descendants of the Greeks.

At the point in their history when Ned comes into their city, they are threatened with destruction by a migrating black army called the M'gai. The Kranois leaders are disunited and cannot organize a successful defense until Ned and a young commander are finally allowed to use the cannon Ned has rescued from the burned slave ship from which he escaped. Meanwhile, Ned meets a young girl of the Kranois, Yvonne, who becomes his wife; and, with the threat of the M'gai over, she joins him on a return voyage to England where, while serving as the Kranois' envoy, he is exonerated of the murder of his friend, the admiral. The true murderers of the admiral, Ned's stepbrother Dennis and his accomplice, are hanged.

The legend of the Kranois is an allegory about preparedness that is Masefield's attack on the division and the divisiveness in England during the 1930s. Always a patriot, he wanted his nation strong and firm especially in the face of growing European totalitarianism; but, unfortunately, few if any reviewers and not many readers seemed to get Masefield's message. Nonetheless, the siege of the city of the Kranois is a particularly effective part of the book. Masefield has of course seen war and described it in *Gallipoli, The Old Front Line,* and *The Battle of the Somme.* How he applies his descriptive powers in the area of land warfare is, for example, seen as he describes the advance of the enemy army:

. . . the army of the M'gai had formed and were advancing on us in line. I counted eight main divisions of them, and reckoned that each contained seven hundred men. The regiments or tribes were each readily distinguished; one wore tall plumes of birds, one the skins of spotted monkeys, one leopards' skins, and so forth. They marched silently and with speed, and halted about a hundred yards from the walls. As they halted, they grounded their spears and long narrow shields. Each man began very gently to tap his white hide shield with his spear hand, till a gentle drumming noise filled the plain. It grew louder and louder, till it rang and roared and echoed. Each drumming man, under his headdress, seemed not less than seven feet tall; each grinned as he drummed, so that the rows of teeth made a white streak down their line. The broad blades of their stabbing spears shone in the sun, and each man glistened with oil. They had a ripple in their walk, a sort of ease and insolence in their bearing. Perhaps few of them had ever seen a city before, and they knew not quite what sort of puzzle it might be. But it was plain that they judged that their spears would soon solve the puzzle. Their chieftains stood in advance of the line; and now, presently, the leaders rode up, dismounted, left their ponies with young bucks who wore scarlet birds as loincloths, and advanced to the parley. The main chief was a short, squat figure, seared all over his chest and arms with the weals of scars, and of enormous physical strength; he was very black. With him was a taller morose-looking savage, not nearly so dark, and certainly thirty years younger. He was the chief of a regiment who wore big green wooden rattles on their arms. Each man in moving made a sort of dry, threatening rattle like that of the rattlesnake. The two men were followed by a Kranish captive, led by two savages. He was to be the interpreter.

The two chiefs advanced towards the gate near which we stood. They moved with insolent ease and mastery, as though all the land belonged to them. While they advanced, and after they had halted, the M'gai beat their shields and hissed. I know no more frightful sound than the one they made, thus. (246-48)

The Latin American and African novels of Masefield are all what some people call "good reading." They are fast-moving tales; they are set in exotic if sometimes improbable places; they create new worlds to visit; and, lastly, they are high romances. In that respect these novels are the products of the poet in Masefield as the sea novels are the product of the sailor in him. Both groups are what we might expect of John Masefield, Poet Laureate of Great Britain. The last two categories of Masefield's novels are less satisfying and less satisfactory.

III   *English Life*

It may be that Masefield placed his greatest hope and expectation as a novelist in his long prose narratives about nineteenth- and twentieth-century England. He deeply loved his country in a most literal sense—he loved the land, the rural people, and the past. His attitudes toward the political institutions were at first guarded; but, as he grew older and more conservative, he regarded these institutions, especially the monarchy, with increasing favor. After World War I, sane man that he was, Masefield could no longer be jingoistic about his country; but he wrote with ever-increasing affection in poetry, fiction, and, later on, autobiography about the England of his childhood and somewhat earlier. His view of the past became more and more romanticized and idealized until his rural England became really a dreamed Paradise instead of an experienced reality.

Masefield's greatest success had, of course, been in the area of verse narratives, particularly those that dealt with rural English life. Masefield hoped to duplicate this success in prose, and the evidence for this intention is the number of characters and places taken from *Reynard the Fox* and *Right Royal* and used in the novels, particularly *The Hawbucks*, which Masefield probably felt was to be his most important work of prose fiction. He wanted to take an area of English country life and encapsulate it in words for all time, as Thomas Hardy did with his Wessex and Arnold Bennett with his Five Towns. Masefield created country people of great credibility, such as Charles Cothill of *Right Royal* and *The Hawbucks*, and old Baldy Hill of *Reynard the Fox*, *The Hawbucks*, and *Eggs and*

Baker. Although the sense of place in his work would often be true, he never achieved the profundity and universality of Hardy or the Balzac-like realism of Arnold Bennett. It is not so much that a dark and foreboding Egdon Heath was beyond Masefield's talent as it was alien to his temperament.

Masefield's first novel of English life, however, preceded his larger plans and even preceded the great verse narratives. Although the novel *The Street of To-day* was published in 1911, the same year as the poem *The Everlasting Mercy*, the reader finds it difficult to envision them as works by the same author; for the novel, which attempts social comment and offers rather shallow psycho-sexual insights, is distinctly inferior as a work of literature to the narrative poem. *The Street of To-day* is the story of a love affair and an unsuccessful marriage between an idealistic man and a neurotic woman. As a study of journalistic life, a life which Masefield knew, the novel is better; and the "landscape" of London, a city which Masefield did not like as a young man, is successful in its view of that city as a great, incurable, cancerous sore crawling with human maggots. In fact, the focus of satire shifts from the incompatibility and sexual antagonism of Rhoda and Lionel Heseltine to the great wasteland of London, to be better dealt with shortly by T. S. Eliot. The modern city was for young Masefield a place so filthy and miserable that it prevented men and women from seeing through the collective degradation to the reality of the beauty of the individual soul. But description is not enough; characterization fails in *The Street of To-day;* and little happens in this stodgy, slow-moving novel. Masefield fumbles either because he was too close to the time, the place, and the people or because he was trying to write the "in" thing rather than following the bent of his own talents. He never returned to contemporary London for the setting of a novel although he would from time to time visit its past, and it would be eighteen years before Masefield would write another novel about English life.

Because *The Hawbucks* (1929) was written just prior to Masefield's laureateship, he may have realized that, as a possible successor to Bridges, he needed to publish an "English" novel; for his last two major works had been *Sard Harker* and *ODTAA*. *The Hawbucks* is set in the fox-hunting district of the West Midlands, the Reynard country; and it contains a love story that seems unable to make up its mind whether to be lighthearted or tragic in a Hardyesque way. The hero is George Childrey, the second son of an established country family. He is called home, after seven years of wandering abroad, to assume responsibility for the family estates after the death of his older brother. He falls in love with the local belle, Carrie Harridew, who is also pursued by all the eligible young men of the district and beyond, including George's younger brother. Miss Harridew, much like Olivia of *Captain Margaret*, with unerring stupidity chooses the worthless younger brother.

Not surprisingly, the climax of the story is a fox hunt. Brokenhearted over his rejection by Miss Harridew, George rides recklessly to a hunt at St. Margarets. With all his senses heightened by his anguish, George is the first rider to see the fox break cover. George leads the hunt for four miles and is drawn into rough and unfamiliar country. When two friends catch up to him to warn him, one, Charles Cothill of *Right Royal*, tries to head George's horse without success; for George is trying to ride into hell. "He had a sudden wave of knowledge from the horse that it was an appalling place: that there was something beyond; but there was not time to think of that. 'If it's the hob of hell,' he cried, 'go over.' Over they went into Stonepits Old Quarry, the horse into deep water, unhurt, and George onto the stone" (321). The story concludes as George, having failed to break his own neck, recovers consciousness and is nursed by Carrie's beautiful but illegitimate half-sister whom he marries. A harsh but fair judgment is that the story, like the horseman, falls flat. The best of the book are the glimpses of country life and the capturing of the spirit of that vanished way. In that respect, there is value in the reading of *The Hawbucks;* for the tapestry of English country life is, in its own way, as much of a record as Masefield's sagas of the sea are records of a way of battle between man and nature not now regularly pursued. *The Hawbucks* is strong in its description of the English landscape; of a fair, a great point-to-point race; and, of course, of the hunts. All of the chief characters and much of the locale are derived from *Reynard the Fox*. Interestingly, although the hunt descriptions are well done in *The Hawbucks*, they never achieve the excitement of the fox hunt in *Reynard the Fox*. The point-to-point race, which occupies twelve pages of *The Hawbucks*, and which is made even more exciting because four of the riders are also competing for the favor of Carrie Harridew, is nevertheless not quite so skillfully presented nor as engrossing as the steeplechase in *Right Royal*. Among those George is racing against is Charles Cothill on a beautiful black: "the black led, Tencombe led, Kilkenny led [George's mount], Muckish led again. Then Kilkenny's effort seemed to grow greater as though he were suddenly become a greater horse: instantly there came a final, swift, fatal sorting out of values. George was past the white post a neck ahead, the black second, Muckish third; and all four horses went careening on for fifty yards before they could come to a canter or pull up" (296).

Eggs and Baker; or, The Days of Trial is plain, homespun Victorian fare, something of a literary throwback. In a small English town during the 1870s, the kind, concerned baker Robert Mansell is inveigled by the unprincipled, professional radical reformer Engels into agitating against slum conditions. The baker loses his shop as his customers desert him, and he later goes to jail for throwing an egg at the chest of a callous judge who condemns men to death merely for poaching. Unfortunately, Masefield does not seem quite willing to take sides in the situation; and the reader is never sure if Masefield is for or against reform. He seems to be for it but to be against reformers. The poachers' trial and the baker's contempt-of-court scene is the best part of a strained and unsatisfying narrative.

The Square Peg; or the Gun Fella is cleverer, better written, and more interesting than its immediate predecessor, *Eggs and Baker*, with which it shares a locale. Not quite a sequel, *The Square Peg* nevertheless is concerned with the twentieth-century descendants of the characters in *Eggs and Baker* and particularly with Robert Mansell, the wealthy, successful businessman descendant of the baker. *The Square Peg*, Masefield's most satirical book, deals with the aspirations of the middle class toward the preserves of the landed gentry, as well as with that traditional subject for romantic poets, modern industry's devouring of the land. This time the horsy set is presented with some hostility, with the exception of Sir Peter Bynd of Coombe, a courteous and sympathetic gentleman of the old school.

Robert Mansell, an intelligent young businessman who is the inventor of the ingenious and inexpensive machine gun Mansell's Deadly Death Rose, buys an ancient estate and remodels it as a home for his bride-to-be and himself. Unfortunately, his fiancée is killed on the day of the wedding, and her loss embitters his subsequent conflicts with the local society folk, who look with contempt and fear upon his plans not only to make an animal sanctuary in that fox-hunting country but to prohibit fox-hunting on his proper-

ty. The irony is delightful; the inventor of Mansell's Deadly Death
Rose, that grinder of human beings, is an animal lover. The local
gentry use underhanded methods to remove him, and they too are
given a going over by Masefield, who, in the tradition of John
Galsworthy and *The Forsyte Saga*, judges individual characters but
refuses to judge a whole society, perhaps because to do so is a futile
effort.

The people of *Reynard the Fox* return in *The Square Peg*, this
time with a social issue at stake. Although fox-hunting is once more
a subject, it surely must have appeared to Masefield's loyal readers
in 1937 that by now they would never know how Masefield truly
felt about that blood sport—and they were right. Still, they must
have enjoyed the effective points made against a provincial
England, previously defended by the establishment poet, and now
presented as considerably spoiled by industrialization and drained
of human vitality by emigration and World War I.

John Masefield's novels of English life are clearly not his most
successful group. His penchant and his talent for detail—qualities
so delightful in depicting ships and shipboard life and so important
to the establishment of a geography like the Sugar States—become
tedious and over-fastidious when applied to the foreground of
nineteenth- and twentieth-century England. Furthermore, as a
novelist with knowledge of the sea, Masefield had no living com-
petitor except Joseph Conrad; but, in treating with English life and
society, Masefield naturally invited comparison with Thomas Hardy, John Galsworthy, Arnold Bennett, Ford Maddox Ford, and D.
H. Lawrence—and Masefield was simply never in that heady
league.

IV   *Medieval Novels*

John Masefield's last three novels in the 1940's were highly
romantic, exotic tales. Two of them, *Basilissa* and *Conquer* take
place in the Byzantium of Justinian, the most glorious emperor of
that great civilization; and the third, *Badon Parchments*, adds to the
Arthuriad. Like his old mentor, Yeats, who died in 1939, Masefield,
now an old man too, was sailing to Byzantium. Inexplicably and
horribly, stupidly and unthinkably, war had come again. Although
he could gird up his loins once more and work for his beloved country as a man, he could not as an artist digest the incredibility of yet
another mass slaughter.

The last novels of Masefield are not successes. These escapist, semihistorical narratives never achieve believable characterization or transcend the narration of historical events. *Basilissa; a Tale of the Empress Theodora* is a whitewash of that woman whom history records as bloodthirsty and depraved but whom Masefield presents as being as good as a governess, besides being clever, talented, and beautiful. The book is pale and without vitality. Masefield completely failed to capture the jeweled splendor, the opulence, and the mosaic-like luxuriousness of Byzantine civilization. He makes the mistake of presenting this story, as well as that of *Conquer*, through the eyes of a "dry official who has little sympathy with any of the wild passions which blazed through the empire. They are good reporting, but they are like black-and-white reproductions of a complex painting."[8]

Conquer: A Tale of the Nika Rebellion in Byzantium is an account of the civil war that nearly destroyed Byzantium in the year 532 and from which the heroic Justinian emerged in complete control. Justinian's character is more convincing than most in this short novel, an exercise in historical reconstruction. As to Empress Theodora, a former courtesan, Masefield remains too much of an old gentleman to face her squarely. Again, no character truly comes to life and the reader leaves the book knowing a little more about the sixth-century history of New Rome but nothing more about life.

Badon Parchments, which is only 150 pages long, is tied to the Byzantine novels through the narrator, John of Cos, an envoy of Justinian and Theodora, who reports to them the events in Britain. Masefield is showing what was happening in Britain when Byzantium was in its golden moment; for the Age of Arthur was a golden period for Britain too. The author is also showing that political intrigue and even military science remain essentially unchanged in many respects from Arthur's Britain to Winston Churchill's.

The character of Arthur, ironically treated as a political pawn, is more successfully drawn than either Justinian or Theodora in the Byzantine novels. Masefield is more comfortable closer to home. Accepting some historical authorities and sources and rejecting others, Masefield places the Battle of Badon in the middle of the sixth century, a generation later than the date 518 A.D. recorded in the *Annales Cambriae*. Arthur is Aurelian, a Romanized Christian king of West Britain, under attack by the heathens of Norfolk and Kent. He initiates a system in which his army is thoroughly reorganized into loyal, company-strength units called "tables," since they are messmates; the best of them share the Roundtable, but the Square, the Pentagon, the Triangle, and others also exist.

The bones of Masefield's disenchantment with some of his less patriotic contemporaries break through when he speaks of traitorous young Britons, who have been deluded into believing that the heathen stood for the worker against the masters, stealing relay horses, cutting down signal posts, burning forage, and otherwise committing acts of sabotage against Britain. The traitors are painted red, banished from their villages, and sent to the heathen who burn them alive for committing the crime of being caught. There are the Red Heathen and the Black Heathen who represent in the slight allegory of this work Communism and Fascism.

Masefield's description of corruption in the medieval government is particularly interesting and pertinent; but, all in all, John of Cos's report to Justinian and Theodora is highly favorable in its analysis of the people of Britain who have a great language, who are valiant in a cause, who are hopeful in despair, and who are generous to the enemy. Nonetheless, Masefield is really covering old ground in *Badon Parchments*, the ground he covered in *Midsummer Night;* and he once more provides the opportunity to compare a scene in a poem and an episode in a novel. This time, both scene and episode concern a battle; and the poem is once more the winner.

V *Novels for Young People*

Although *Badon Parchments* ended Masefield's career as a novelist, his novels written for young people must not be ignored, for this work contains some of his best stories. No disparagement is meant to Masefield in the thought that as a novelist he may have been best suited for the writing of young people's books, for "His peculiar blend of zest and gravity, of relish and intense concentration, together with his love of the technicalities of any craft, make an ideal equipment for a children's writer."[9] And, after all, storytelling was his forte and simplicity a fact and a virtue in his work. He deeply loved children and animals; and the heroes of his best adult books are young, adventurous Englishmen. When they are a few years younger, they are the heroes of his books for boys and girls. In the earlier books for the young, *A Book of Discoveries*, *Martin Hyde*, *Lost Endeavor*, and *Jim Davis*, Masefield was writing as much for his own children as for all the others. Three of these novels were published in the year Lewis Masefield was born and

Judith was five, and the fourth in Lewis's first year of life. Today, *Jim Davis*, *The Midnight Folk*, and *A Box of Delights* are still in print in Puffin paperbacks and are widely read by young people throughout the English-speaking world.

A Book of Discoveries, *Martin Hyde*, and *Lost Endeavour* were all first published in 1910. *A Book of Discoveries* is the tale of two small boys who love to explore and to play such traditional games as pirates and wild Indians. Trespassing on the property of a neighbor, Mr. Hampden, they are surprised by him, and all three become good friends. Mr. Hampden, an archaeologist and a naturalist, often takes the lads camping, and, when he takes them for a whole week on a hill that was once a stronghold of ancient Britons, they make remarkable discoveries in a British Roman cave and much excitement and fun follow. There is a great deal of seaman's lore and chartmaking in the book as Masefield again brings into use his own nautical education. The novel is a good story for a bright ten-to-twelve-year-old child, although a modern youngster would find it somewhat less sensational than the fare to which he is now accustomed.

Martin Hyde, the Duke's Messenger is a galloping first-person narrative that really succeeds in bringing history to life for youngsters. Martin, a seventeenth-century orphan, is nearly thirteen years old, when, in the fateful year of 1685, he is taken to London to live with his uncle. Because of his disobedience, he is confined to the upper story of his uncle's home. Making an escape through the window of his room, Martin winds up in the presence of the Duke of Monmouth who, with his accomplices, is conspiring against King James II. Because the secrets Martin has overheard are too important and too dangerous to allow his release, Martin is given his choice between indefinite imprisonment or service in Monmouth's illegal cause. He joins the rebels and becomes their messenger to The Netherlands. On his expeditions his path often crosses a brave young girl's, the dark and mysterious Aurelia Carew, a spy in King James' service. She grows to care for the younger boy; and, when the rebellion comes in arms to the West Country of England and fails, she saves Martin's life while the duke and his supporters are sent to the Tower of London to be beheaded.

Martin Hyde is as exciting, as plausible, and as carefully crafted as any of Masefield's novels; and its characters lack pretensions. The hero is not a perfect or preachy do-gooder but a wrong-headed, frightened, semidelinquent who makes the wrong choices but is worth saving. He is far more easily identified with by young boys than the typical Robert Louis Stevenson or the G. A. Henty boy-hero. Furthermore, there is an equally courageous and a far wiser young woman to whom girls can relate in this successful early novel of John Masefield. It should be noted that Masefield's first fox hunt is not in *Reynard the Fox* but in *Martin Hyde* (282 - 84); and Masefield seemed at that early moment almost committed to the fox: "The horsemen paused for a second, surprised at the sudden sharp turn; but they followed the hounds' lead, popping over the fence most nimbly, not waiting to look for my tracks in the banks of the hedge. They streamed away after the fox, to whom I wished strong legs. I knew that with two young hounds they would never catch him, but I hoped that he would give them a good run before the sun killed the scent" (284).

Rightfully, *Lost Endeavour* has been much praised.[10] The story is a hauntingly sad and richly written narrative about a schoolboy, Charles Harding from Blackheath, who, along with his French schoolmaster, Teodoro Mora, is kidnapped in the year 1690; both are to be sold as slaves in Virginia. The highly charged story relates their separation and subsequent meeting in Virginia, their escape, and their Indian and pirate adventures. The schoolmaster, nick-named Little Theo, turns into a mystic and a fanatic; but he also becomes the leader of a buccaneer band who is frantically obsessed with the quest for a treasure trove. Charles grows old and wise beyond his years, for he is haunted by the fear that he may become hardened by criminal life. Charles and Theo only get a glimpse of the treasure in one brilliantly described scene. That is the lost endeavor. Theo succeeds in becoming the sacred ruler of the Indian tribe that worships the treasure horde.

Masefield takes us to Latin America again as he did in *Captain Margaret*, and such an imaginative flight becomes a frequent com-mutation in the novels of the Sugar States and is generally a sign that the author is in very good form. Masefield's description of the exotic succeeds here as it does in *Captain Margaret*. But what is most interesting in *Lost Endeavour* is the fact that the book is not a story of childhood innocence; rather, it is a surprisingly mature narrative about a youth's growing awareness of the presence and the nature of evil. Because this story presents questions rather than provides answers, *Lost Endeavour* is a book that precedes but is quite similar in tone to Richard Hughes' *A High Wind in Jamaica: or the Innocent Voyage* and to William Golding's *Lord of the Flies*.

Jim Davis, the most popular of the books for young people that Masefield wrote in this early period, is quite the opposite of *Lost Endeavour*. Taking place during the Napoleonic War, the story is about a ten-year-old boy who goes to live with his uncle on the Devon coast. Having observed smugglers in action, Jim is eventually captured by them; and, because he knows too much, they force him to join their band. After a trip to France, Jim returns home with the smugglers and is eventually rescued after several additional adventures. *Jim Davis*, a simple book, reads quickly. The vocabulary is carefully designed for teen-agers, and an atmosphere of the early nineteenth century is skillfully evoked.

The Midnight Folk and its sequel *A Box of Delights* are two excellent fantasies of and for childhood. They are such magical books and are so far above the average books for children that a reader may wonder why no adult cult has developed about them. *The Midnight Folk* is about a boy named Kay Harker, one of Sard's clan. His governess, Daisy Pouncer, is a witch who must be routed with the help of "the midnight folk," a company of friendly animals that includes a distinguished rat who calls himself a "marine cellarman." Kay has learned from his guardian, Sir Theopompus, of the treasure ship lost by his great-great-grandfather, Captain Harker of the *Plunderer*. That august personage comes to Kay at night, perhaps in a dream, to tell him more of the mystery. Kay is committed to try to find the treasure before the evil Abner Brown and his crew of witches do so; and "the midnight folk" finally help him solve all. Because *The Midnight Folk* is a young boy's dream in which his village, his house, and the everyday external objects of his life take on a shimmering magical new meaning, it is very much a poet's book for children, as is its sequel.

The Box of Delights, or When the Wolves Were Running is the story of an older Kay Harker who, on his way home from school, falls asleep on the train, and then his adventures begin. He meets an old Punch and Judy man who entrusts him with the magic Box of Delights with which Kay can go back in history and see Roman legionaries on the march, men in furs fighting wolves, and great Troy smoking from its last siege. Old King Cole is there in the guise of Cole Hawlings, and he and Kay must work hard and face dangers together to make sure that the villainous Abner Brown, in disguise as Father Boddledale, head of a theological college, does not steal the box and sabotage the midnight Christmas service of the cathedral. In the nick of time, they rescue the true clergy, and the cathedral service proceeds until Kay is awakened by the sound of great music. The characters—Kay, Cole, Abner, and the dear witch Daisy Pouncer—are magnificent; the fantasy is sharp and lucid; and no condescending attitude appears toward children. This work and its predecessor are books which men and women read in their youth, remember all their days, and use to judge the imaginative quotient of their own lives. For Masefield, they were flights of creative fancy which gave him and his daughter Judith, who illustrated *The Box of Delights*, enormous satisfaction and pleasure. Masefield's *Martin Hyde* has been much appreciated by the librarian-critic of children's literature, Lillian H. Smith, of the Toronto Public Library, and a 1976 Newberry award-winning English writer, Susan Cooper, indicates that Masefield's *The Midnight Folk* and *Box of Delights* played a part in awakening her imagination.

John Masefield was not a great novelist. His prose fiction narratives, although they gave great pleasure to tens or perhaps hundreds of thousands of readers, are seldom analyzed by critics or recalled by scholars. Some of the books for young people have continued and will continue to be read for a long time. *The Bird of Dawning* and *Victorious Troy* will hold a position in the twentieth-century English novel similar to that held by Masefield's early lyrics like "Sea-Fever" and "Cargoes" in twentieth-century English poetry; read, reread, loved, and sometimes memorized, they are at most only passingly alluded to in the works of scholars and critics.

CHAPTER 7

The Sword and the Pen: Historical, Critical, and Autobiographical Prose

THE canon of Masefield's non-fiction prose writings is staggeringly vast. In the area of literary criticism alone, besides hundreds of book reviews and articles, he wrote substantially about Shakespeare, Chaucer, the Augustan writers, Robert Herrick and other seventeenth-century poets, Elizabethan theater, Synge, Yeats, John Ruskin, William Blake, John Keats, Percy Bysshe Shelley, and others. His autobiographical prose writing includes these books: *In the Mill* (1941), *New Chum* (1944), *So Long to Learn* (1952), and *Grace Before Ploughing* (1966). His writings concerning nautical history such as *Sea Life in Nelson's Time* (1905), *On the Spanish Main* (1906), *The Wanderer of Liverpool* (1930), and *The Conway* (1933) are excellent and respected works.

Towering above these histories is *Gallipoli* (1916), one of four which Masefield wrote about World War I and World War II. Besides this prose epic, one of the greatest studies of British men in war ever written, he also wrote *The Old Front Line* (1917), *The Battle of the Somme* (1919), and *The Nine Days Wonder* (1941), the story of the evacuation at Dunkirk. These works must be considered first; for, if the business of a poet laureate is to express and embody in his writing the highest public values of his nation, Masefield earned with *Gallipoli* the laureateship and with *The Nine Days Wonder* "he justified the appointment many times over."[1]

I Men at War: From the Dardanelles to Dunkirk

To comprehend today the impact that *Gallipoli* had on the English-speaking world and how long that impact lasted is difficult.

From 1918 to 1939, British school children heard passages of the book read to them annually on Armistice Day, for *Gallipoli* served the twofold function of glorifying the courage, fortitude, and endurance of the British soldier in modern warfare and of deploring the terrible, obscene waste of war.[2] In a way, and for a generation, *Gallipoli* became the British *Song of Roland*. Written in the high style of the epic, it served the religion of patriotism and was universally read. Indeed, this Masefield work is most frequently found in used book sales and on Salvation Army shelves in Britain and in North America. No lover of English language and literature should ignore this book, for *Gallipoli* is the masterpiece of its own subgenre: battle history. As Erich Maria Remarque's *All Quiet on the Western Front* is the great work of fiction of World War I and as Robert Graves' *Goodbye to All That* is the finest biography of a soldier in that war, so *Gallipoli* is the best battle history that emerged from the holocaust of 1914-1918.

An example of the accolades *Gallipoli* received is this passage from the first full-length study of Masefield's work, W. H. Hamilton's *John Masefield: A Critical Study* (1922): "*Gallipoli* is a book to strike the critical faculty numb and hush the heart of the hearer. For an age—aye, for ever on the earth so far as we can dream it—it will be read and gloried in afresh and heads will be bowed and the tears of strong men shed at every telling. It is as yet too sacred for applause."[3]

Gallipoli is the prose epic for an heroic military disaster—the 1915 campaign at the Dardanelles that was devised by Sir Winston Churchill, then First Lord of the Admiralty, and that was designed to separate Turkey from the other Central Powers by dividing European Turkey from its greater Asian part. When British and Anzac troops seized a beachhead on the Gallipoli peninsula but were ultimately unable to hold it against spirited Turkish counterattacks, they were forced to evacuate after enormous loss of life. This campaign was the first great amphibious operation of modern warfare; the next one was to occur at Guadalcanal in 1942. Churchill resigned in disgrace, went to the front lines as an infantry colonel where he fortunately survived, and Americans in general thought that the campaign had been an exercise of sheer stupidity. It wasn't; the idea was sound even if the planning and the execution were faulty.

Masefield was visiting the United States on behalf of the British war effort at the beginning of 1916. Having been at Gallipoli, he was continually barraged with questions about the campaign and with criticisms of the way the operation had taken place. Returning to England, Masefield decided to justify Britain's military way to the Americans:

When there was leisure, I began to consider the Dardanelles Campaign, not as a tragedy, nor as a mistake, but as a great human effort, which came, more than once, very near to triumph, achieved the impossible many times, and failed, in the end, as many great deeds of arms have failed, from something which had nothing to do with arms nor with the men who bore them. That the effort failed is not against it; much that is most splendid in military history failed, many great things and noble men have failed. (3-4)

Gallipoli was a hard book for Masefield to write in one particular respect; for, like most English intellectuals before the war, he had been strongly pacifistic and had expressed his feelings against war in *Multitude and Solitude* and in *The Street of To-day,* Along with so many others, he changed his views and supported Great Britain in the war with Imperial Germany; and only a few of the pre-war pacifist intellectuals and artists such as George Bernard Shaw and Bertrand Russell did not. Nonetheless, *Gallipoli,* despite its patriotism, neither supports war as a means of settling disputes nor exalts the military. Rather, it celebrates the common soldier who falls into a pool of his own blood and sweat on Chocolate Hill or who sails away in exhaustion and defeat from Anzac Cove. The history contains a geographical description of the battle area, an explanation of the campaign plans, a detailed account of the campaign, and an exposition of the reasons which made its failure inevitable.

Masefield, who was consciously writing the British epic of the war, preceded each section of the book with an appropriate quotation from the *Song of Roland.* His prose is so superb that the reader cannot doubt that this quickly written book was formed in the fires of inspiration and dedication. For example, the expedition leaves the port of Mudros, in Lemnos:

Ship after ship, crammed with soldiers, moved slowly out of harbour, in the lovely day, and felt again the heave of the sea. No such gathering of fine ships has ever been seen upon this earth, and the beauty and the exaltation of the youth upon them made them like sacred things as they moved away. All the thousands of men aboard them, gathered on deck to see, till each rail was thronged . . . . In a few hours at most, as they well knew, perhaps a tenth of them would have looked their last on the sun, and be a part of foreign earth or dumb things that the tides push. Many of them would have disappeared forever from the knowledge of man, blotted from the book of life none would know how, by a fall or chance shot in the darkness, in the blast of a shell, or alone, like a hurt beast, in some scrub or gully, far from comrades and the English speech and the English singing. And perhaps a third of them would be mangled, blinded or broken, lamed, made imbecile or disfigured, with the colour and the taste of life taken from them, so that they would never more move with comrades nor exult in the sun. And those not taken thus would be under the ground, sweating in the trench, carrying sandbags up the sap, dodging death and danger, without rest or food or drink, in the blazing sun or the frost of the Gallipoli night, till death seemed relaxation and a wound a luxury. But as they moved out these things were but the end they asked, the reward they had come for, the unseen cross upon the breast. All that they felt was a gladness of exultation that their young courage was to be used. They went like kings in a pageant to the imminent death. (43-45)

This passage contains a great sense of the Homeric and of the medieval saga traditions in its praise of human courage, determination, and sacrifice. *Gallipoli* was Masefield's best opportunity to express his perennial belief that victory of a moral kind could be snatched from physical defeat. Those who survived, Allies and Turks, were greater men for their experience: they became the archetypes of manhood; they became the images of history:

On all the roads, on the plain, which lay white like salt in the glare, and on the sides of the gullies, strange, sunburned, half-naked men moved at their work with the bronze bodies of gods. Like Egyptians building a city they passed and repassed with boxes from the walls of stores built on the beach. Dust had toned their uniforms even with the land. Their half-nakedness made them more grand than clad men. Very few of them were less than beautiful; whole battalions were magnificent, the very flower of the world's men. They had a look in their eyes which those who saw them will never forget. (220)

Masefield's ability to describe war scenes, those ultimate moments of human action, is truly remarkable: he captures the movement, the sound, the smell, the very air of conflict. He paints magnificent detailed cycloramas of war in a manner seldom equalled and never surpassed:

Looking out from the upper dugouts one saw the dusty, swarming warren of men, going and coming, with a kind of swift slouch, carrying boxes from the beach. Mules and men passed, songs went up and down the gullies, and were taken up by those at rest, men washed and mended clothes, or wandered naked and sun reddened along the beach, bathing among dropping bullets. Wounded men came down on stretchers, sick men babbled in pain or cursed the flies, the forges clinked, the pile drivers beat in the balks of the piers, the bullets droned and piped, or rushed savagely, or popped into a sandbag. Up in the trenches the rifles made the irregular snaps of fire-crackers, sometimes almost ceasing, then popping, then running along a section in a rattle, then quickening down the line and drawing the enemy, then pausing and slowly ceasing and beginning again . . . . Then the dust settled, the ruin was made good, and all went on as before, men carrying and toiling and singing, bullets piping and the flies settling and swarming on whatever was obscene in what the shell had scattered.

Everywhere in those positions there was gaiety and courage and devoted brotherhood, but there was also another thing, which brooded over all, and struck right home to the heart. It was a tragical feeling, a taint or flavour in the mind, such as men often feel in hospitals when many are dying, the sense that Death was at work there, that Death lived there, that Death wandered up and down there and fed on Life. (222-24).

Gallipoli was no defeat in Masefield's mind. Like the United States Marines at Chosan in the Korean War, the British had triumphed in defeat. Or the poet at least made it so for English history, as Homer did chanting of the Trojans to the Greeks. In the end Masefield, like an Anglo-Saxon chronicler, puts words into the mouths of the Turkish enemy, whom he has say of the British:

They did not win, but they came across three thousand miles of sea, a little army without reserves and short of munitions, a band of brothers, not half of them half-trained, and nearly all of them new to war. They came to what we said was an impregnable fort on which our veterans of war and massacre had laboured for two months, and by sheer naked manhood they beat us, and drove us out of it. Then rallying, but without reserves, they beat us again and drove us further. Then rallying once more, but still without reserves, they beat us again, this time to our knees. Then, had they had reserves, they would have conquered, but by God's pity they had none. (244).

No writer ever knows which if any of his work will endure, but some do write with a weather eye set on posterity. Sometimes Masefield wrote for the future; sometimes he clearly did not; but *Gallipoli*, if any of his work, is for all time.

Rather than military epics like *Gallipoli, The Old Front Line: or, The Beginning of the Battle of the Somme* and its sequel *The Battle*

of the Somme are pure historical essays. When Masefield was re-
quested by high-ranking officers to write the history of this battle as
he had written the history of the Dardanelles campaign, he was not
given the access to the plans and to the unit diaries, which account
the day-to-day activities of a force, as he had been for Gallipoli; but
the casualties may have been so stupendous that the military
authorities were afraid to release the facts to the public. Masefield
analyzes the campaign, the topography, and eventually the results.
To do so, he interviews many Commonwealth soldiers and uses
their comments and stories; and, in the end of *The Battle of the
Somme*, he pays a moving tribute to them all. In these two
historical essays, Masefield is at his best in describing the curiously
blind, mole-like world of the trench soldier. Indeed, Masefield's
ability to describe men at war is undiminished, as is indicated by
the conclusion to *The Old Front Line:*

In our trenches after seven o'clock on that morning, our men waited under
a heavy fire for the signal to attack. Just before half-past seven, the mines at
half a dozen points went up with a roar that shook the earth and brought
down the parapets in our lines. Before the blackness of their burst had
thinned or fallen, the hand of Time rested on the half-hour mark, and along
all that old front line of the English there came a whistling and a crying.
The men of the first wave climbed up the parapets, in tumult, darkness,
and the presence of death, and having done with all pleasant things, advanced across the No Man's Land to begin the Battle of the Somme. (128)

The Nine Days Wonder; The Operation Dynamo is Masefield's
brief day-by-day description from May 26 through June 3, 1940, of
the evacuation of Allied forces from Dunkirk and the rescue of over
three hundred thousand men. In this book, which contains only
fifty-six pages and four short poems of thanks to the fallen, the subject is one for which Masefield—the lover of England, the romancer
of ships and sailors, and the believer in victory through defeat—was
truly destined. Masefield went to writing this work like an old cam-
paigner to the trumpet call of his last battle; for he saw his beloved
sailors—not only the men of the Royal Navy, but the merchantmen,
the yachtsmen, and the ferrymen—join together in one magnificent
English-style improvisation in order to rescue their army and save
their nation. For Masefield, Operation Dynamo "was the greatest
thing this nation has ever done." (10)

Masefield's historical prose in *The Nine Days Wonder* shows
evidence of his continual crisping, tempering, refining, and harden-
ing since *Gallipoli*. Understatement is the stylistic key:

Among the remarkable feats of the day must be mentioned that of Able-Seaman S. Palmer, in the thirty-foot motor-yacht, *Naiad Errant*. Putting into the beach in the surf, she was rushed and swamped. She was then washed ashore. He refloated her. He had no crew, save one stoker, but he gathered a British N.C.O. and eight soldiers and with these put off for England. The engine was not working well and at last broke down. He then broke up the wood fittings of the yacht, into paddles, and induced the eight soldiers to paddle. He reached Dover safely. (32)

Just as the Dardanelles campaign had not driven Turkey from the war, the British Expeditionary Force of 1940 did not save the Low Countries and France. Just as the British were driven from Gallipoli in 1916, they were driven from Dunkirk in 1940. For Masefield, both of these were great epic victories of the English spirit; and he was right. Endurance and overcoming are the keel and the ribs of this spirit, for what other people could make of the London blitz, the bombing of their greatest city, a victory? Because Masefield understood these aspects of the national character so fully and expressed them so finely in *Gallipoli* and in *Nine Days Wonder*, the English deeply loved him, just as he loved his people. To Masefield, Dunkirk was meaningful, for:

The Nation rose to the lifting of the Armies as to no other event in recent times. It was an inspiration to all, to feel that will to save running through the land. The event was as swift as Life; no possible preparation could be made; the thing fell suddenly, and had to be met on the instant. Instantly, in reply to the threat, came the will to help from the whole marine population of these islands. Word passed that the armies were shipwrecked on the sands; at once the lifeboats put out, and kept plying as long as there was anyone to lift.
    Our Army did not save Belgium; that is a little matter compared with the great matter, that it tried to. In the effort, it lost thirty thousand men, all its transport, all its guns, all its illusions; it never lost its heart. (53)

Appearing so early in the war, *The Nine Days Wonder* set a standard of unhysterical, restrained, factual writing that was generally adhered to by subsequent journalists and historians. For example, the prose style of the American naval historian of World War II, Samuel Eliot Morison, is very reminiscent of Masefield's account of the Dunkirk evacuation. With *The Nine Days Wonder*, John Masefield "broadened the Laureate tradition"[4]: he had become the laureate of the people as well as that of the monarch.

II   *Other Historical Writing*

The remainder of Masefield's historical work was about maritime history and about ships important in his life. In *Sea Life in Nelson's Time* (1905), an historical essay, Masefield describes the brutally hard conditions under which British seamen labored in the Napoleonic period. He delves deeply into ship rigging and design as well as into ordnance and tactics. Most importantly, however, Masefield acknowledges, and bids his countrymen acknowledge, that British wealth, prosperity, and security are to be attributed to the long line of anonymous men who sailed before the mast and who underwent great suffering under martinets who were themselves prisoners of an unbending system. A sensitive essay, it is properly concerned with placing the source of a nation's freedom and wealth in perspective.

On the Spanish Main: or, Some English Forays on the Isthmus of Darien. With a Description of the Buccaneers and a Short Account of Old Time Ships and Sailors (1906) is a work of impressive research. Masefield, who claimed not to be a scholar,[5] had in truth the ability, the patience, and the talent for excellent historical research. *On the Spanish Main* deals with the English presence in the Caribbean during the buccaneer period, the battles of English captains such as Morgan with the Spanish, the organization of buccaneer crews, and the capture of Panama and Porto Bello. Although the research involved in this book provided a watershed for *Captain Margaret* and other novels, it remains a major work of Caribbean history.

Masefield writes splendidly about individual ship's histories, particularly *The Wanderer of Liverpool* (1930) and *The Conway* (1933, revised 1953). While he was a merchant marine cadet on the *Conway*, he watched for the beautiful barque *Wanderer*, which had been launched on August 20, 1891, and he saw her limp back to Liverpool with courage and splendor in defeat after having been severely mauled in a storm. As noted earlier, the vessel, which figured so importantly in his poetry and prose fiction, became in the moment of her return his permanent symbol of the glory of noble failure. Very naturally, he wrote her history in prose and verse, dedicating this beautifully illustrated book "to all old wanderers." Masefield lovingly describes the wooden figurehead of a beautiful woman that is gazing dead ahead—a figure that is surely the muse of his creativity. Of the *Wanderer*, he speaks of the height of her masts, of the spread of her sail, of the wood of each spar, of the weight of her ballast of coal, and of the cheers, the glorious cheers from the shore, that would send beauty on her way. Masefield describes each voyage of the ship until while anchored on the morning of April 14, 1907, in the Elb River, Germany, the *Wanderer* was struck and sunk by a steamer. Her end is described in forty-six pages of verse that Masefield summarized with the thought:

> Herself is not there, being Beauty Eternal, alive,
> She wanders the waters of thought, past disasters, past hates,
> Past the world's disapproval, across the black seas of despair,
> And on, beyond anguish to havens of peace when she brings
> Hope, Mercy and Courage, all gentle and beautiful things. (103)

The *Conway* was Masefield's school ship, and the book *The Conway* (1933) is actually a history of a school for British Merchant Marine officers. Although this institution is similar to the United States Merchant Marine Academy, the British boys were much younger; and they lived, studied, and trained entirely aboard an old man-of-war afloat in the Mersey at Liverpool. Three different *Conway* ships existed from the school's establishment in 1858 until the last one ran aground in April, 1953. The book is of particular value to those who are interested in English professional training and to others who realize that the British Merchant Marine in the nineteenth-century and in the first half of the twentieth century was highly instrumental in making Britain the wealthy and powerful nation that she was. Masefield revised the book in 1953 to bring the story of the *Conway* to its end and to have an opportunity as an old seaman-writer to express his gratitude to his school.

III *Literary Criticism*

When considered all in all, Masefield's contribution to literary criticism was quite large; for, as noted earlier, he published several short volumes, many individual essays, introductions to anthologies, and collections, book reviews, and newspaper articles. His three most important contributions in this area are, however, *William Shakespeare* (1911), *Chaucer* (1931), and *Thanks Before Going* (1946). When Masefield wrote his *William Shakespeare* as the second work in a series called The Home University Library, his criticism created no stir. In retrospect, this work is important not only because it is a very wise and useful introduction to Shakespeare but because it shows that Masefield possessed "an imagination capable of measuring the heights of Shakespeare's work. The insight of certain passages in it is Shakespearean."[6]

Masefield considers each play by summarizing the plot and by then providing the reader with direct, authorative, definitive commentary and insight. In fact, Masefield's observations show him to be the possessor of considerable knowledge of the theater, a quality all too lacking in early twentieth-century Shakespearean critics. Masefield responded strongly to Shakespeare's patriotism in the history plays; and these works, interestingly enough, influenced his prose, particularly his historical prose, in that the reader cannot help but sense the nationalistic attitudes of Shakespeare being expressed by Masefield in *Gallipoli* and *The Nine Days Wonder*. The essence of *Henry V* and the "band of brothers" is there as well as Lear's "Men must endure."

As for Masefield's *Chaucer*, which originated as the Leslie Stephen Lecture spoken at Cambridge on March 2, 1931, no scholar or critic has ever said so much about Chaucer in so few words. The book is only thirty pages long, but Masefield establishes with the precision of a poet the mood and climate of Chaucer's time, the motivations that moved the medieval poet to write, and the eternal values of England's first great literary artist. Masefield does this with charm and wit—and makes slight digs at the academic community in the process.

In *Thanks Before Going*, a slender study of the poetry of Dante Gabriel Rossetti, Masefield belatedly acknowledged his own debt and that of the other poets of the Georgian generation to Rossetti who had died when Masefield was a child but whose poetry was one of Masefield's early companions. As a young poet, Masefield had sought those who had known Rossetti in order to learn about his idol. In his book, a work of clarification, not profundity, Masefield succinctly and sensitively explicates and comments on the canon of Rossetti's poetry.

Masefield was not a great literary critic. Indeed, literary criticism, like his historical writing, was only a sideline. His criticism, however, is characterized by highly individual insights and valid iconoclasm. Because, he respected his own judgment, he always took the pronouncements of the giants of criticism with a grain of salt.

IV   *Biographical Writings*

In his early sixties, Masefield began to think more and more about the events and the formulative incidents of his youth. He was escaping from World War II, and he was evaluating, summing up, and trying to find the meaning of his life. This mood resulted in a series of autobiographical writings, and one of them is in verse, *Wonderings: Between One and Six Years* (1943). It contains some fine poetry in a Wordsworthian way and some evocative childhood perceptions; but, to the continued frustration of a Masefield biographer, almost no biographical facts. The other writings are in prose: *In the Mill* (1941), *New Chum* (1944), *So Long to Learn* (1952), and *Grace Before Ploughing: Fragments of Autobiography* (1966).

In the Mill is Masefield's account of the two years, 1895-1897, that he spent working in a Yonkers carpet factory after leaving his ship in New York City and before returning to England to pursue a writing career. A gentle book, it is full of kind reminiscences about America and Americans; but of particular importance to a study of Masefield is his listing of the early, influential reading he did before the age of twenty: Chaucer, of course, but also Keats, Shelley, Sir Thomas Malory, Swinburne, and others. In sharply focusing on a two-year period of his life, Masefield reveals himself as an affable, sensitive, quiet young man who was liked by most people, who was easy to help, but who was not a prodigy or an early talent. He learned the craft of writing by his own hard work during his years of apprenticeship to this trade, as well as to the seaman's trade.

"The mill" itself emerges as a background character, and it is interesting to note how the poet, in his first and last personal contact with industrialism, saw the factory. With the delight of a naturalist, Masefield describes its operation and organization. It is not cruel or kind, ugly or beautiful, soul destroying or protective; it simply *is*, as a mountain *is* or a river *is*. But the things men make, even carpets, are a wonder and a joy. Masefield did not resent the mill or its owners, nor do the other workers in the book seem to do so. They did not feel exploited; they seemed to feel that the mill was giving them fair wages and that it was a matter of honor and dignity to return to it their best efforts.

It is amazing to consider this attitude since the period that Masefield was writing about was a time of great unemployment and of some of the bitterest labor struggles in American history—the America of Upton Sinclair's *The Jungle*. The reader wonders if most workers at that time of industrial revolution and of the founding of the modern American labor union movement were as complacent, as satisfied, and as untouched by the surface storms of revolution as Masefield indicates. Or the reader ponders whether or not Masefield's memories, some forty-five years after the facts, planed away the sharp edges of reality and varnished over the rawness of the truth. Perhaps the answer is that Masefield was always a Romantic; he saw reality through romantic eyes. His strange and beautiful innocence that was so often noted by those who knew him provided the rose tint to his perspective on the worker and the factory.

The style of *In the Mill* is so smooth, so easy flowing, so unbroken that it is a particularly pleasant autobiography to read. It and *New Chum* are books so well written that they would be of interest and importance even if their author had not been a major poet in his lifetime, but had continued to pursue a career either at sea or in the mill. In fact, the reader merely regrets that Masefield was willing to write so candidly about only such short periods of his life.

New Chum, a remarkably precise and detailed account of the first term of Masefield's education in H.M.S. *Conway* from September through December, 1891, lacks the expected historical elements in an autobiography, such as dates, places, and names of people (they are hidden behind titles, nicknames, or initials). *In the Mill,* Masefield's first autobiographical prose work, deals with only two years of his youth, but *New Chum* focuses even more narrowly on a few months. Critics and scholars who thought that Masefield might be presenting a full autobiography in several volumes began to despair that they would never have the full story, and they were right. As one reviewer questioned, "Is Mr. Masefield's life quite momentous enough to justify the immense length at which he is telling it?"[7] Masefield's autobiographical writing, either by design or by accident, never proceeded beyond his childhood and his youth.

However, none of those considerations detract from the charm and fascination of *New Chum*. Masefield manages in an unforced way to recollect and reconstruct, through the eyes of a thirteen-year-old boy, that first term on the training ship *Conway* in which he became a sailor and a teller of stories. The ultimate significance of *New Chum* for the reader of Masefield is that the author discloses how he, in the service of a dear older friend who enjoyed listening to stories, began the role of storyteller; and, although Masefield would leave the water, he would never leave the word.

New Chum is a paean to the wonder and the joy of life—to the hard, sometimes even cruel life of an apprentice sailor. The reader shins up the ratlines to the crosstree and surveys with a perceptive view the wonderful world of shipping:

I never failed to be stirred by the view southward from that now vanished dock. You could not see the River, for sheds, buildings, and our beloved Baths were in the way; instead of the river, you saw a kind of lightening in the sky in which a gull or two might shine; you knew that the River was there, with all its glory of beauty. I had not dreamed that any place could be so beautiful; I went towards it, knowing that I should see a new view of it, under an early morning sun. (267)

By implication, the book is also critical of the nature of apprentice training because what Masefield learned on the *Conway* was better preparation for a seaman's life in Nelson's time than for Masefield's era, the age of steam.

So Long to Learn recounts Masefield's memories of life before embarking on the *Conway* and includes some ground covered in *Wonderings*. Jumping over previous work like a checkers player, Masefield also recalls his second term on the *Conway*, his life in New York City prior to the period covered in *In the Mill*, his meeting with Yeats and his life in London around 1900, his early attempts at writing stories and drama, his first involvement in the theater, and, oddly enough, at the end of his book, his hopes and expectations for English literature. This *potpourri* of prose is Masefield at his most disjointed, but the reader finds many worthwhile passages of insight, comment, and observation, as well as many vague and dull parts. Masefield again posits the importance of esthetics in life when he says: "With a decent shelter and enough food, neither very hard to win, the effort to create beauty, in the praise of undying beauty, must bring gladness . . . ." (180). In *So Long to Learn*, Masefield attempts to tell "all that has seemed important to me in my effort to become a writer and teller of tales" (181). He also promises to tell the rest of his life "in work still unfinished" (181). All that came of that resolution was one last brief work only ninety pages long that was published just before the poet died.

Grace Before Ploughing; Fragments of Autobiography again tells
about his childhood at Ledbury and romances a rural England that
disappeared with World War I. In simple, uncluttered prose he
recounts what seem to be memories of memories. Masefield un-
derlines the continuity of human life in many ways, as when he
remembers talking to a man who had seen a mail-coach that had
brought news of the victory at Waterloo. His memories are no
longer connected by time, only by place: Ledbury, Herefordshire,
England, somewhere in Europe, the world, the universe.

Most of the memories, in fact, are memories of the pleasures of
childhood: the smithy, water flowing in a canal, a hunt passing,
painting a picture with a lot of red paint, and, perhaps particularly
significant, witnessing the local company of brightly uniformed
militia volunteers marching to Ledbury Church where the young
boy (Masefield) had first implanted in him a sense of service to God,
Queen, and country. "It was at one of these church parades that I
first understood the power of a great service on the human heart."
(52)

As personal history, Masefield's efforts in the area of autobiography are disappointing. As the history of a poet's imagination,
such efforts are somewhat more rewarding but do not cover enough
of his lifetime. As interesting and informative reading—that kind of
autobiographical writing that reconstitutes a time and a place—only
In the Mill and *New Chum* succeed; but the second work is more
successful than the first one. Of Masefield's forest of historical,
critical, and autobiographical prose, one work stands out above all
others; indeed, it rivals any single Masefield accomplishment in all
the other genres he attempted. That work is *Gallipoli;* the English
Iliad for two generations of this century and perhaps for other
generations in the time to come.

CHAPTER 8

Achievement and Summation

" "THE Poet Laureate's sixty years of creative writing has qualities of epic and spiritual significance elsewhere unmatched," opined G. Wilson Knight in 1960.[1] In fact, John Masefield, who was a successful, widely-published, creative writer for nearly seventy years, was one of the most prolific writers in the history of English literature. Volume, of course, is no criterion of value; but the student of Masefield must be impressed with the wide-ranging albeit "intermittent genius" of the man.[2] He was the complete man of literature: a poet, a novelist, a dramatist, an historian, a propagandist, a literary critic, a reviewer, and an essayist on almost every subject from agriculture to women's suffrage. True, his work was uneven; but "Uneveness, provided the output is large, is often a sign of genius."[3] Masefield like any other artist, however, must be judged primarily in terms of his best work; and Masefield's best work—the sea lyrics, the long narrative poems, and his epic history—should have earned for him a permanent place in the Pantheon of twentieth-century English writers.

I Impact on Early Twentieth-Century Poetry

Masefield is "peculiarly a poet who must be taken for his positive virtues rather than for his shortcomings . . . . For if he does not finish all of his poems to our satisfaction, neither does he finish any of them to death. He is neither precious nor fashionably obscure. His poetry is perfectly comprehensible to any intelligent person who can read; it has nothing to do with cults and illuminati."[4] Between 1911 and 1945, John Masefield was the most widely read and admired English poet. In his long verse narratives such as *The Everlasting Mercy, The Widow in the Bye Street, Dauber,* and *Reynard the Fox,* he had managed to bring back to English poetry a mixture of vivid brutality and textured beauty that is one of its most human and enduring characteristics. In these works he developed powerful descriptions of landscapes and of seascapes that complemented the gusto of his stories, thus making the Georgian movement in poetry—of which he was a part by proximity and not by choice or age—seem more vital than it really was. Indeed, "What Masefield did, about 1910, was to take the old ballad tradition which told a fast-moving, action-filled story in a couple of hundred lines or less, and (using a slower-moving measure to modify the gallop of ballad into something nearer a canter for the longer form) expand those couple of hundred lines into something more like two thousand: the short story of the ballad became the long-short story—the *conte*— of the Masefield narratives. But it lost nothing in dramatic interest; it never dragged . . . ."[5]

The unexpected excitement and controversy over subject matter and language generated by *The Everlasting Mercy* in 1911 benefited poets everywhere and incidentally provoked a host of imitations in England and in America where Vachel Lindsay and Robert Frost were particularly aware of the impact that Masefield was making in popularizing realistic subject matter in verse. Poetry, alas only for a brief moment, had returned to the people and had stirred a general interest. Sophisticated critics looked down their noses while clergymen quoted *The Everlasting Mercy* from pulpits. When it had all died down, Masefield was recognized not as the man who had brought dirty words into poetry but as a master English storyteller in the tradition of Chaucer and as the best writer of the narrative poem since William Morris. He conveyed stories "in the most pleasurable and memorable form, without emphasis on moral, political or religious issues or issues personal to the poet. That is not to say that moral, political, religious or personal themes do not exist in his work; only that they are not emphasized by a didactic intention."[6]

Masefield's best protagonists, to the delight of the general audience, were ordinary men and women: country folk, gentry, the poor, the sailors, the private soldiers, the outcasts, the farm girls, the real English boys and "navvies." Masefield wrote about Phillip of Spain, Pompey of Rome, and Theodora of Constantinople, but these were not his most memorable heroes and heroines. In every genre he undertook, the finest characters were ordinary humans: the young English sailors of the novels and Dauber, the rankers of *Gallipoli,* and two valiant animals: Reynard and Right Royal. Thus Masefield was ever true to the promise he made in 1902 with "A

Consecration": the slave, the burdened man, the sailor, the chantyman—"Of these shall my songs be fashioned, my tales be told."

II *Vitality, Clarity, Optimism*

It may seem terribly trite and naïve in 1977 but one must
acknowledge that John Masefield was consciously and dedicatedly
on the side of Good. He was, as a writer and a human being,
without viciousness, jealousy, and rancor; he was so loving and so
positive about life that his readers are almost overcome by his passion for the beauty in the human soul, for the grace and nobility in
animals, for the glory of growing things, and for the grandeur of
man-made things like ships. As has been rightly observed, "He has
sided always with the weak against the strong. The right things
have moved him, whether to anger or joy. Sensitive, gentle, and
brave, he has found his mainspring in love of life and compassion
for all that live it."[7]

Since Masefield was a writer, not a philosopher, it is perhaps
useless to attempt to locate a philosophical position in his work;
therefore, those who seek consistent and original metaphysics and
logic in literature, will probably find Masefield's poetry bromidic.
Instead, his is a poetry of dogged vitality; his optimism is forever at
war with the destructive or paralytic pessimism in the world and in
himself; and his is resultantly a philosophical portrayal of life as a
struggle against an insentient and brutal evil that is expressed in the
poem "Watching by a Sickbed":

> And all day long the stone
> Felt how the wind was blown:
> And all night long the rock
> Stood the sea's shock;
> While, from the window, I
> Looked out, and wondered why,
> Why at such length
> Such force should fight such strength.

Action not ideas is Masefield's forte; and, beyond his early
attempt to protest against scientific fatalism and his early search for
some system in which he could locate a place for his intuition of
beauty, he avoids such arguments as the existence of the soul, life
after death, the nature of reality, and the existence of God. When
he serves his purposes artistically by using belief in any form or

manner, he simply does so without justifications; in fact, he even accepts incarnation as the monarch in *King Cole* or the ship-spirit in *Sard Harker*. Otherwise, he is resigned to personal investigation and observation. In "The Isle of Voices," one of his last poems, he says that ". . . nothing is forbidden./ Not even Peace, but all the doors are hidden/ And iron-locked, and we must find the key."

Masefield's most typical work was surely *Reynard the Fox*. It is a vigorous, vital, precise, patient, and dramatic poem of such length and high intention that it must be ranked as a masterpiece of English poetry. It is a poem of Masefield's that is "the most technically accomplished, the widest in range of characterization and action."[8] As a verse narrative, *Reynard the Fox* contains the most characteristic action in Masefield's work: a chase; for that or the race is the primary source and the architectonic of action in much of Masefield's best or most serious work. To cite some examples, Masefield uses the chase in *The Everlasting Mercy*, the steeplechase race in *Right Royal*, the clipper-ship race home in *The Bird of Dawning*, the race and the hunts in *The Hawbucks*, the escape from pursuers in *Captain Margaret*, *The Taking of the Gry*, and *Dead Ned*. Even in his histories, the race and its concomitant tension are present, particularly in *The Nine Days Wonder*, where British seamen race against time and the German enemy to save the Allied army. In this spine of horizontal action, moving in sometimes friendly sometimes deadly competition toward a goal, with its accompanying thrills and tensions, lies the secret of Masefield's popularity. His dedication to visualized action parallels the rise of the cinema during the first half of the twentieth century.

III   *Interpreter of English Life*

In a writer as prolific and as varied as Masefield, it is almost impossible to discern some single overriding theme or intention. Yet one does seem to emerge in Masefield's canon. It may not have been consciously thought out but, long before he became Poet Laureate, John Masefield began to develop as one of the most important interpreters of English life in the late nineteenth and early twentieth century. He did so through theme, through character, through setting, and through his minute attention to trades, crafts, contemporary historical events, and rural society. He underscored his Englishness with his study and attention to Chaucer,

Shakespeare, Malory, and other aspects of the Arthuriad. In retrospect, Masefield's appointment as Poet Laureate in 1930 does not seem at all surprising. He was the most English of all living English writers, in part because he was the most comprehensibly English. Although Hardy was supreme in the depiction of the nineteenth-century English countryman, although Kipling was supreme in his portrayal of the Englishman as colonizer, and although Conrad was noted for his Englishman at sea, Masefield dealt with all of these aspects of English life—and he did so competently. Of course, Masefield's *Hawbucks* cannot compare with Hardy's *Return of the Native*, or his Dauber as a tragic English sailor with Conrad's Lord Jim; but the significant fact is that Masefield attempted it at all and did so with considerable success. As to Kipling, Masefield shares subjects, never philosophy; for Masefield is neither an imperialist nor an advocate of European supremacy. The saint of England for Masefield is the self-sacrificing Christian noble, St. George—not the acquisitive John Bull.

Working within the traditional forms of English literature, Masefield made a unique contribution in that he created a significant body of good English sea poetry, not a little of which is still read today outside of the classroom. For a nation of sailors, English sea poets have been few and far between. Masefield stands above all others in this respect; and, even in prose, "With Conrad he shares the honor of having written more realistically and more convincingly about sea life than almost any writer."[9]

Masefield's long verse narratives, though not so widely read as the sea poems, seem destined to be remembered as either fine examples or as the last examples of the genre. At the moment, there seems to be no interest on the part of English or American poets to return to the form. *The Everlasting Mercy, Dauber*, and *Reynard the Fox* will continue to be anthologized and dealt with in the critical histories of twentieth-century British poetry. Masefield's relationship to and his derivation from Chaucer continue to be important as men seek to establish the continuity of an art form. Although Masefield's post-1930 poetry, with its evident diminution of self-criticism, will not be considered important, two novels, *The Bird of Dawning* and *Victorious Troy* are read, if not by critics and scholars, by those who love tales of adventure at sea.

Therein lies the essence of Masefield. What he wanted to become most of all—what he consciously planned for his literary future in

1911 or perhaps earlier—was a master storyteller. The art of storytelling was for him an honorable, traditional, bardic occupation. He believed that people loved to hear and read good stories, and he set out to write good stories in verse. When that power somewhat failed him, he turned to prose. John Masefield succeeded in his search for his art.

Toward the end of his life he turned to reminiscences and the reworking of old experiences in his autobiographical writings. In that sense, he turned old age to an advantage, for readers could not help but be fascinated by recollections of the youth of any man who lived so long, wrote so well, and remembered so much. His own generation particularly honored and revered him for writing *Gallipoli,* one of the great books of World War I and perhaps the best history of a single campaign ever penned. The book went through eight editions almost immediately, for it seemed to offer some meaning and some solace to all the mindless slaughter of that terrible war from which Europe never truly recovered. *Nine Days Wonder* provided some proud comfort for the next generation of Englishmen in a very dark hour.

John Masefield was not a man born to privilege or to power. His formal education was meager. He never studied in a university or even in a secondary school. He was trained for the hard life of a deck officer in the merchant service. In his youth, he was a wanderer and a gatherer of experiences. Painfully and methodically, he educated himself for a life in literature. Considering the origins of this orphan child and the odds against him, his accomplishments were magnificent. As in the case of Shakespeare, Masefield's fellow writers almost without exception viewed him with respect and affection. He was never jealous nor vindictive. For a moment in his artistic life he brought a new vitality to English poetry and stimulated interest when and where it was sorely lacking. His beloved England honored him as it had honored few other living artists.

Although time and tastes eventually passed him by, he was never forgotten in his lifetime, and although the critics deserted him, the people never did. John Masefield was a traditionalist; he did not wish to change English poetry; in fact, he went back to Chaucer for inspiration. He made no innovative contribution to the form of the novel as did James Joyce or Virginia Woolf; he was content to tell a good story in the old-fashioned way. But because of his excellent renderings of such traditional English forms as the lyric and the narrative, "it is hard to see how the future can reject him as one of the foremost English poets of the first half of the twentieth century without at the same time rejecting the whole tradition of English poetry."[10]

Notes and References

Chapter One

1. L. A. G. Strong, *John Masefield* (London, 1952), p. 5.
2. *So Long To Learn* (New York, 1952), p. 4.
3. Stanley P. Chase, "Mr. John Masefield: A Biographical Note," *Modern Language Notes*, XL (1925), 85.
4. *So Long to Learn*, p. 16.
5. *Wanderings* (London, 1943), p. 16.
6. Ibid., p. 11.
7. *Recent Prose* (London, 1932), p. 210.
8. Ibid.
9. *So Long to Learn*, p. 8.
10. Ibid., p. 10.
11. F. Berry, *John Masefield: The Narrative Poet* (University of Sheffield, 1967), p. 2.
12. *The Ledbury Scene As I Have Used It In My Verse* (Hereford, 1951), p. 4; reprinted in *St. Katherine of Ledbury* (London, 1961), p. 66.
13. *Recent Prose* (New York, 1933), p. 154.
14. *New Chum* (New York, 1945), pp. 40 - 41.
15. Ibid., p. 168.
16. Ibid., p. 169.
17. Ibid., p. 170.
18. Ibid., p. 176.
19. Muriel Spark, *John Masefield* (London, 1953), p. 37.
20. *New Chum*, p. 152.
21. Ibid., pp. 184 - 85.
22. Spark, p. 38.
23. *So Long to Learn*, pp. 50 - 51.
24. Ibid., p. 52.
25. Ibid., p. 53.
26. Ibid., p. 59.
27. Ibid., p. 53.
28. Ibid., p. 54.
29. Ibid., p. 67.
30. Ibid.
31. Louise Townsend Nicholl, "John Masefield in Yonkers," *The Bookman* ([New York] January, 1919), p. 544.
32. *In the Mill* (London, 1941), p. 95.
33. Ibid., p. 101.

34. Ibid., p. 97.

35. Sir William Rothenstein, *Men and Memories* (New York, 1931), I, 373.

36. *So Long to Learn*, p. 87.

37. Ibid., p. 94.

38. See Fraser Drew, "The Irish Allegiances of an English Laureate: John Masefield and Ireland," *Éire-Ireland*, III (1968), 24-34.

39. Masefield, *Some Memories of William Butler Yeats* (Dublin, 1940), p. 10.

40. Ibid., p. 19.

41. Corliss Lamont, *Remembering John Masefield* (Rutherford, New Jersey, 1971), pp. 27 - 28.

42. John Masefield, "Preface," in Lewis Masefield, *The Passion Left Behind* (New York, 1947), pp. 1 - 19.

43. "Preface," *Poems: Complete Edition with Recent Poems* (New York, 1953), p. viii. Unless otherwise noted, all quotations of Masefield's verse are from this edition.

44. "Preface," *Prose Plays* (New York, 1925), pp. x - xi.

45. Henry W. Nevison, *John Masefield: An Appreciation* (London, 1931), p. 31.

46. "Preface," *Poems*, pp. viii - ix.

47. Herbert Palmer, *Post-Victorian Poetry* (London, 1938), p. 128.

48. Strong, pp. 18 - 19.

49. John Cournos, "A Visit to John Masefield," *Independent* (New York), Sept. 5, 1912, p. 534.

50. Ibid., p. 537.

51. Ibid., p. 538.

52. Nevison, p. 5.

53. "St. George and the Dragon," *The War and the Future* (New York, 1918), pp. 10 - 11.

54. Fraser Drew, "John Masefield: Interpreter of England and Englishmen," unpublished doctoral dissertation (University of Buffalo, 1952), p. 337.

55. *Gallipoli* (New York, 1917), p. 3.

56. Drew, "John Masefield," p. 337.

57. *Recent Prose*, pp. 99 - 101.

58. Lamont, pp. 106 - 07.

59. Ibid., pp. 28 - 30.

60. Lamont, p. 26.

61. Ibid.

62. Ibid., p. 103.

63. Spark, p. 58.

Chapter Two

1. W. H. Hamilton, *John Masefield: A Critical Study* (London, 1922), p. 25.

2. Palmer, p. 124.

3. Cecil Biggane, *John Masefield: A Study* (Cambridge, England, 1924), p. 2.

4. Spark, p. 77.

5. Amy Lowell, *Poetry and Poets* (New York, 1930), p. 188.

Chapter Three

1. Berry, p. 2.

2. Spark, pp. 88 - 89.

3. *Chaucer* (New York, 1931), pp. 12 - 13.

4. Ibid., p. 11.

5. M. Fisher, *John Masefield* (London, 1963), p. 26.

6. Drew, "John Masefield," p. 80.

7. Berry, p. 17.

8. Ibid., pp. 2 - 5.

9. Robert Lynd, *Old and New Masters* (London, 1919), p. 154.

10. Strong, p. 19.

11. Lynd, p. 151.

12. Lowell, p. 189.

13. Strong, pp. 21 - 22.

14. J. Middleton Murray, *Aspects of Literature* (Freeport, New York, 1970), p. 150.

15. *Recent Prose*, p. 144.

16. Ibid., p. 154.

17. Ibid., p. 155.

18. *Dauber and Reynard the Fox* (London, 1962), p. 78.

19. John W. Cunliffe, *English Literature in the Twentieth Century* (New York, 1933), p. 302.

20. Lawrence Mason, review of *Enslaved*, *The New Republic* (Aug. 18, 1920), p. 341.

21. *Chaucer*, p. 28.

Chapter Four

1. Ashley H. Thorndike, "The Great Tradition," *The Dial* (Chicago), Feb. 8, 1919, p. 120.

2. Biggane, p. 33.

3. Lionel Stevenson, "Masefield and the New Universe," *The Sewanee Review*, XXXVII, No. 3 (July, 1929), 340 - 41.

4. Anonymous, "Twentieth Century Poets" (review), *New York Times*, Jan. 31, 1915, p. 24.

5. "A Memory," *A Tarpaulin Muster* (London, 1907), pp. 112 - 13.

6. Gilbert Thomas, *John Masefield* (London, 1932) pp. 81 - 82.

7. *Poetry* (New York, 1932), p. 38.

Chapter Five

1. "Preface," *The Collected Plays of John Masefield* (New York, 1919), p. x.

2. Anonymous, "Mr. Masefield as a Playwright" (review of *The Collected Plays of John Masefield*), *The Nation*, CVIII (Mar. 22, 1919), 432.

3. "Playwriting," *Recent Prose*, p. 105.

4. Ibid., pp. 106-07.

5. Anonymous, "Mr. Masefield as a Playwright."

6. Newman I. White, "John Masefield—An Estimate," *The South Atlantic Quarterly* (1927), p. 193.

7. "Playwriting," *Recent Prose*, p. 106.

8. Alden Whitman, "Found Muse in Yonkers" (obituary), *New York Times*, May 13, 1967, p. 22.

9. "Preface," *The Collected Plays of John Masefield*, p. ix.

10. C. E. Montague, *Dramatic Values* (Garden City, New York, 1925), p. 202.

11. Ibid., p. 199.

12. "Preface," *The Collected Plays of John Masefield*, p. x.

13. Ibid.

14. Ibid.

Chapter Six

1. Spark, p. 184.

2. G. Wilson Knight, "Masefield and Spiritualism," *Mansions of the Spirit: Essays in Literature and Religion*, ed. George A. Panichas (New York, 1967), p. 263.

3. Spark, p. 179.

4. Gilbert Highet, *People, Places, and Books* (New York, 1953), p. 51.

5. Fisher, p. 46.

6. Spark, pp. 182, 184.

7. Ibid., p. 183.

8. Highet, p. 151.

9. Strong, pp. 29 - 30.

10. See Spark, p. 172; Fisher, pp. 48 - 49.

Chapter Seven

1. Strong, p. 31.

2. Fisher, p. 29.

3. Hamilton, p. 138.

4. Kenneth Hopkins, *The Poets Laureate* (London, 1954), p. 190.

5. *Chaucer*, p. 1.

6. Strong, p. 8.

7. Harold Hobson (review of *New Chum*), *Christian Science Monitor,* April 14, 1945, p. 14.

Chapter Eight

1. Knight, p. 259.
2. Strong, p. 5.
3. Ibid.
4. White, p. 199.
5. Hopkins, p. 189.
6. Spark, p. 13.
7. Strong, p. 35.
8. Spark, p. 21.
9. J. Edward Mason, *John Masefield* (Exeter, England, 1938), p. 31.
10. White, p. 200.

Selected Bibliography

PRIMARY SOURCES

1. Collections
Collected Plays of John Masefield. New York: Macmillan, 1919.
Selected Poems. London: Heinemann, 1922.
Collected Poems. London: Heinemann, 1923.
A Book of Prose Selections. London: Heinemann, 1950.
Poems: Complete Edition with Recent Poems. New York: Macmillan, 1953.

2. Separate Works
Salt-Water Ballads. London: Grant Richards, 1902.
Ballads. London: Elkin Mathews, 1903.
A Mainsail Haul. London: Elkin Mathews, 1905. (Fiction)
Sea Life in Nelson's Time. London: Methuen, 1905. (Historical essay)
On the Spanish Main: Or, Some English Forays on the Isthmus of Darien. With a Description of the Buccaneers and a Short Account of Old Time Ships and Sailors. London: Methuen, 1906. (Historical essay)
A Tarpaulin Muster. London: Grant Richards, 1907. (Fiction)
Captain Margaret: A Romance. London: Grant Richards, 1908. (Fiction)
Multitude and Solitude. London: Grant Richards, 1909. (Fiction)
The Tragedy of Nan and Other Plays. London: Grant Richards, 1909.
The Tragedy of Pompey the Great. London: Sidgwick and Jackson, 1910. (Drama)
Martin Hyde: The Duke's Messenger. Boston: Little, Brown, 1910. (Fiction)
A Book of Discoveries. London: Wells Gardner, Darton, 1910. (Fiction)
Lost Endeavour. London: Thomas Nelson and Sons, 1910. (Fiction)
William Shakespeare. London: Williams and Norgate, 1911. (Critical essay)
The Everlasting Mercy. Portland, Maine: Smith & Sale, Printers, 1911. (Verse.)
Jim Davis. London: Wells Gardner, Darton, Ltd., 1911. (Fiction)
The Street of To-day. New York: Dutton, 1911. (Fiction)
The Widow in the Bye Street. London: Sidgwick & Jackson, 1912. (Verse)
The Story of a Round-House and Other Poems. New York: Macmillan, 1912.
Dauber: A Poem. London: Heinemann, 1913.
The Daffodil Fields. New York: Macmillan, 1913. (Verse)
Philip the King and other Poems. London: Heinemann, 1914.

John M. Synge: A Few Personal Recollections with Biographical Notes. Dublin: The Cuala Press, 1915. (Essay)

The Faithful: A Tragedy in Three Acts. London: Heinemann, 1915.

Good Friday and Other Poems. New York: Macmillan, 1916.

Sonnets and Poems. Letchworth: Garden City Press, 1916.

The Locked Chest; The Sweeps of Ninety-Eight: Two Plays in Prose. Letchworth: Garden City Press, 1916.

Gallipoli. London: Heinemann, 1916. (History)

Lollingdon Downs and Other Poems. New York: Macmillan, 1917.

The Old Front Line. New York: Macmillan, 1917. (Historical essay)

The Cold Cotswolds. Cambridge, England; reprinted from *The Cambridge Magazine*, 1917. (Verse)

A Poem and Two Plays. London: Heinemann, 1919. ("Rosas"—"The Locked Chest"—"The Sweeps of Ninety-Eight")

St. George and the Dragon. London: Heinemann, 1919. (Essays. Lectures delivered in America.)

The Battle of the Somme. London; Heinemann, 1919. (Historical essay)

Reynard the Fox: or, The Ghost Heath Run. New York: Macmillan, 1919. (Verse)

Enslaved and Other Poems. London: Heinemann, 1920.

John Ruskin. Bembridge School: Yellow Sands Press, 1920. (Essay. Lecture delivered at the Ruskin Centenary Exhibition at the Royal Academy, 1919.)

Right Royal. New York: Macmillan, 1920. (Verse)

King Cole. London: Heinemann, 1921. (Verse, with drawings by Judith Masefield)

A Foundation Day Address. Bembridge School: Yellowsands Press, 1921. (Essay)

The Dream. London: Heinemann, 1922. (Verse, illustrated by Judith Masefield)

Berenice: A Tragedy, Translated from the French of Jean Racine. London: Heinemann, 1922. (Drama, a translation into English verse)

Esther: A Tragedy, Adapted and Partially Translated from the French of Jean Racine. London: Heinemann, 1922. (Drama, an adaptation and partial translation into English verse)

Melloney Holtspur. London: Heinemann, 1922. (Drama)

King Cole and Other Poems. London: Heinemann, 1923.

The Taking of Helen. London: Heinemann, 1923. (Fiction)

A King's Daughter: A Tragedy in Verse. New York: Macmillan, 1923.

Recent Prose. London: Heinemann, 1924. (Essays, new and revised edition 1932).

Shakespeare & Spiritual Life. Oxford: Clarendon Press, 1924. (Essay. The Romanes Lecture, 1924.)

Sard Harker. London: Heinemann, 1924. (Fiction)

With the Living Voice: An Address by John Masefield Given at The First

General Meeting of The Scottish Association for the Speaking of Verse, 24th October 1924. London: Heinemann, 1925. (Essay)

The Trial of Jesus. London: Heinemann, 1925. (Drama)

ODTAA. New York: Macmillan, 1926. (Fiction. The title is made up from the initial letters of the popular saying: "One Damn'd Thing After Another.")

Sonnets of Good Cheer. London: Mendip Press, 1926. (Private printing)

Tristan and Isolt: A Play in Verse. London: Heinemann, 1927.

The Midnight Folk. London: Heinemann, 1927. (Fiction)

The Coming of Christ. New York: Macmillan, 1928. (Drama)

Midsummer Night and other tales in Verse. London: Heinemann, 1928.

Easter: A Play For Singers. New York: Macmillan, 1929.

The Hawbucks. New York: Macmillan, 1929. (Fiction)

South and East. London: The Medici Society, 1929. (Verse)

The Wanderer of Liverpool. New York: Macmillan, 1930. (Essay and Verse. An account of the voyages of the barque Wanderer, together with "A Masque of Liverpool" and other poems.)

Chaucer. New York: Macmillan, 1931. (Essay. The Leslie Stephen Lecture for 1931.)

Minnie Maylow's Story and Other Tales and Scenes. London: Heinemann, 1931. (Verse)

Poetry. New York: Macmillan, 1931. (Essay. A Lecture given at the Queen's Hall, London, on October 15, 1931.)

A Tale of Troy. London: Heinemann, 1932. (Verse)

The Bird of Dawning. London: Heinemann, 1933. (Fiction)

End and Beginning. New York: Macmillan, 1933. (Drama)

The Conway from Her Foundation to the Present Day. London: Heinemann, 1933. (Essay. A history of the training ship Conway.)

The Taking of the Gry. London: Heinemann, 1934. (Fiction)

A Box of Delights: or, When the Wolves were Running. London: Heinemann, 1935. (Fiction)

Victorious Troy: or, The Hurrying Angel. London: Heinemann, 1935. (Fiction)

A Letter from Pontus and Other Verse. London: Heinemann, 1936.

Eggs and Baker: or, The Days of Trial. New York: Macmillan, 1936. (Fiction)

The Square Peg: or, The Gun Fella. London: Heinemann, 1937. (Fiction)

Dead Ned: The Autobiography of a Corpse. London: Heinemann, 1938. (Fiction)

Live and Kicking Ned: A Continuation of the Tale of Dead Ned. London: Heinemann, 1939. (Fiction)

Some Memories of W. B. Yeats. New York: Macmillan, 1940. (Biographical essay)

Basilissa: A Tale of the Empress Theodora. New York: Macmillan, 1940. (Fiction)

In the Mill. New York: Macmillan, 1941. (Autobiography)

Conquer: A Tale of the Nika Rebellion in Byzantium. New York. Macmillan, 1941. (Fiction)

Guatama the Enlightened and Other Verse. New York: Macmillan, 1941.

The Nine Days Wonder: the Operation Dynamo. London: Heinemann, 1941. (Essay. On the Evacuation of the British and French Forces from Dunkirk in 1940.)

Natalie Masie and Pavilastukay: Two Tales in Verse. New York: Macmillan, 1942.

Land Workers. London: Heinemann, 1942.

Wonderings: Between One and Six Years. London: Heinemann, 1943. (Verse)

New Chum. London: Heinemann, 1944. (Autobiography. An account of the author's first term on board the training ship *Conway.*)

I Want! I Want! London: National Book Council, 1944. (Essay. The National Book League Second Annual Lecture.)

A Macbeth Production. London: Heinemann, 1945. (Essay)

Thanks Before Going: Notes on some of the Original Poems of Dante Gabriel Rossetti. London: Heinemann, 1946. (Essay)

Badon Parchments. London: Heinemann, 1947. (Fiction)

Thanks Before Going, with Other Gratitude for Old Delight, including "A Macbeth Production" and Various Papers not before printed. London: Heinemann, 1947. (Essays)

A Play of St. George. New York: Macmillan, 1948.

On the Hill. New York: Macmillan, 1949. (Verse)

St. Katherine of Ledbury. London: Heinemann, 1951. (Essays)

So Long to Learn. London: Heinemann, 1952. (Literary autobiography)

The Bluebells and Other Verse. London: Heinemann, 1961.

Old Raiger and Other Verse. London: Heinemann, 1964.

In Glad Thanksgiving. London: Heinemann, 1966. (Verse)

Grace Before Ploughing: Fragments of Autobiography. New York: Macmillan, 1966.

SECONDARY SOURCES

1. Bibliographies

HANDLEY-TAYLOR, GEOFFREY, comp. *John Masefield, O.M.: The Queen's Poet Laureate, A Bibliography and Eighty-First Birthday Tribute.* London: Crambrook Tower Press, 1960. Includes notes on various Masefield collections.

NEVINSON, HENRY WOODD. *John Masefield: An Appreciation, Together With a Bibliography.* London: Heinemann, 1931.

SIMMONS, CHARLES HERBERT. *A Bibliography of John Masefield.* New York: Columbia University Press, 1930. Also lists works on Masefield. (Errata and emendata, including Masefield's book reviews in

Manchester Guardian, by Fraser Bragg Drew, papers of the Bibliographical Society of America, LIII, 1959.)

2. Books

BERRY, FRANCIS. *John Masefield: The Narrative Poet*. Sheffield, England: Univ. of Sheffield, 1967. A succinct appreciation of Masefield's major narratives. Excellent perspective on the poet's contribution written just after he died.

BIGGANE, CECIL. *John Masefield: A Study*. Cambridge, England: W. Heffer & Sons, 1924. Heavy-handed praise of a coming writer.

DREW, FRASER B. "John Masefield: Interpreter of England and Englishmen." Unpublished dissertation, University of Buffalo, 1952. Available from University Microfilms, Ann Arbor, Michigan. A comprehensive study of Masefield's work according to subjects. Difficult to use because it has no index.

————. *John Masefield's England: A Study of the National Themes in His Work*. Cranbury, New Jersey: Associated University Presses, Inc., 1973. An abridgement of his doctoral dissertation.

FISHER, MARGERY. *John Masefield*. London: Bodley Head monograph, 1963. Belatedly attempts to interest young readers in the old Laureate. Excellent reading for a high school or college freshman research paper.

HAMILTON, WILLIAM HAMILTON. *John Masefield: A Critical Study*. London: George Allen & Unwin Ltd., 1922. First book-length critical study.

LAMONT, CORLISS. *Remembering John Masefield*. Rutherford, N.J.; Fairleigh Dickinson University Press, 1971. Fascinating exchange of letters between Masefield and the Lamont family. Offers more insight into Masefield's later years and values than any other work.

MASON, JOHN EDWARD. *John Masefield*. Exeter, England: [A. Wheaton & Co. Ltd.] The Paternoster Press, 1938. Some insights into Masefield's productivity in his middle years.

SPARK, MURIEL. *John Masefield*. London, P. Nevill, 1953. Superb critical evaluation of Masefield's narrative poetry and adventure novels. Very fair to Masefield. The author is unwilling to gloss over Masefield's literary vices as she praises his literary virtues.

STRONG, LEONARD ALFRED GEORGE. *John Masefield*. London: published for the National Book League and the British Council by Longmans, Green & Co., 1952. A good, brief overview of Masefield's achievement.

THOMAS, GILBERT. *John Masefield*. London: Thornton Butterworth, 1932. Superficial overview of the work of the new Poet Laureate.

3. Selected Articles

COURNOS, JOHN. "A Visit to John Masefield," *The Independent* (New York), Sept. 5, 1912, 533-38. A very early and interesting interview with

Masefield just after the publication of *The Everlasting Mercy* and *The Widow in the Bye Street*. The author, an American journalist, traveled to Masefield's home and observed the developing writer in his environment.

DREW, FRASER BRAGG. "The Irish Allegiances of an English Laureate: John Masefield and Ireland." *Éire-Ireland*, III, 4 (1968), 24 - 34. Documents the relationship of Masefield to Yeats and Synge. Also points out his interest in the Irish theater and in Irish country life. Makes much of the fact that Masefield's wife was Irish.

KNIGHT, GEORGE WILSON. "John Masefield: An Appreciation." *John Masefield, O. M.: The Queen's Poet Laureate.* Ed. Geoffrey Handley-Taylor. London: The Cranbrook Tower Press, 1960, pp. 9 - 11. Short, pithy evaluation of Masefield's narrative skill.

————. "Masefield and Spiritualism." *Mansions of the Spirit: Essays in Literature and Religion.* Ed. by George Andrew Panichas. New York: Hawthorn Books, 1967, pp. 259 - 88. Extols Masefield's clarity and simplicity as well as the spiritual values in his work.

LOWELL, AMY. "John Masefield." *Poetry and Poets.* New York: Houghton Mifflin, 1930, pp. 187 - 209. Positive evaluation of characterization in *Reynard the Fox.*

MONTAGUE, CHARLES EDWARD. "Mr. Masefield's Tragedies." *Dramatic Values.* Garden City, N.Y.: Doubleday, Page, 1925, pp. 197 - 206. Indicative of the positive reception given to the literary value of Masefield's plays in contradistinction to their more limited public acceptance.

MURRY, JOHN MIDDLETON. "The Nostalgia of Mr. Masefield." *Aspects of Literature.* Freeport, N.Y.: Books for Libraries Press, 1970, pp. 150 - 57. Faint praise for Masefield's narrative achievements.

STEVENSON, LIONEL. "Masefield and the New Universe." *The Sewanee Review*, XXXVII (1929), 336 - 48. Most serious study of Masefield's metaphysics ever undertaken.

STURGEON, MARY C. "John Masefield." *Studies of Contemporary Poets.* New York: Dodd, Mead, 1916, pp. 197 - 216. Masefield's narratives as interpreted from the viewpoint of faith and religion.

WHITE, NEWMAN IVEY "John Masefield—An Estimate." *The South Atlantic Quarterly* (1927), 189 - 200. Considering the date, an extremely perceptive evaluation of Masefield indicating the low worth of his novels and plays relative to the poetry. The author realizes that Masefield's poetry will make or break his ultimate critical reputation.

WILKINSON, MARGUERITE. "Poets of the People: A Discussion of War and Poetry by John Masefield" (An interview with Masefield). *The Touchstone* (New York), March, 1918, pp. 587 - 93. Extremely florid, drippy, and overgenerous view of Masefield's work until 1918. Interesting interview with Masefield in which the poet predicts a postwar Romantic movement.

Index

(The works of Masefield are listed under his name)